ELECTRIC KILNS
for ceramics

A MAKER'S GUIDE TO SUCCESSFUL FIRING

Jo Davies

ELECTRIC KILNS
for ceramics

A MAKER'S GUIDE TO SUCCESSFUL FIRING

THE CROWOOD PRESS

CONTENTS

PREFACE

This book has been written from my point of view as a ceramicist with a working knowledge of ceramic kiln-firings. The style and format is based on my practice, which includes the production of a porcelain design range including tableware, lighting and vessels, as well as teaching wheel throwing. Importantly for this book I also ran a kiln-firing service in East London for around twelve years until 2019. My ceramics degree at Bath School of Art and Design and my Master's in Ceramics & Glass at the Royal College of Art have heavily informed the information in this book but the content is also based on countless conversations with fellow professionals over the years who I owe a great deal and are too many to name. The book includes some Maker Profiles from ceramicists whose work I consider interesting and who illustrate the use of kilns to create unique and beautiful work. Their profiles concentrate on ways that they use their kiln to create their work, including unusual approaches that break some of the normal rules, which are written about in this book. This is because, whilst this book aims to give a structure to work from, it is by no means a doctrine and I would encourage rule-breaking to push innovation forward, create new work and make new discoveries.

Throughout my time offering a kiln-firing service I often came into contact with my customers' misunderstandings, particularly those who were only just starting out, around kilns and their function within ceramics. I became familiar with commonly overlooked details (which, when ignored, can have disastrous results) and even the problematic idea that ceramics is collectively one subject with a simple set of rules that are easily quantifiable. Many of these conversations have been the foundation on which I have based the presentation of information in this book.

Throughout I have attempted to put across the need to test results ahead of time, not because of a slavish bid for discipline, but in an attempt to encourage experimentation and the honing of ideas alongside a structure. If there is one lesson in ceramics, it is to always give yourself more time to do something than you think.

At the start of my own journey, when I was learning to work with clay, many of the ceramics books I was directed towards used scientific language and cadence, as if it wasn't an artform I was working with but a science. To a person who is of a creative disposition, and interested in arriving at the making as fast as possible, this was frustrating. The presentation of ceramics as a science was not helpful for me at that stage. Having said this, I do know that a deep understanding through these means can be extremely elucidating for many, but at a later stage. At all times during the writing of this book I have attempted to take into account the creative mindset and tried to arrive at each main point as soon as possible.

In order to be as inclusive to all creative perspectives who wish to work with ceramics, I have also chosen to speak about ceramic 'objects' and 'ceramicists' for the majority of the time rather than 'ware', 'pottery' or 'potter'.

This book aims, for the beginner, to take you through each stage, adding to your knowledge with each subsequent chapter in a way that will be helpful for practical application; it is designed to be read by this type of reader from start to finish for an understanding of electric-kiln firings. For more knowledgeable readers the text can also be used as a reference book to be dipped in and out of as needed.

The firing of kilns will have many factors at play, including external ones affecting the decision-making of the people running them, so some of these considerations are also sometimes discussed in the book. These issues can include anything from ecology, economy, professional deadlines and local politics.

Overall the book has been written to be as understandable as possible with little to no knowledge assumed although, as mentioned above, if coming to this book with little knowledge of kiln firings please take care to read it from the beginning in order to build your knowledge in a way that will make sense of later chapters.

Lastly, all advice in this book should be used in conjunction with the technical specification of the materials you are using, individual manufacturers' advice for the equipment and kilns being used, as well as relevant professional advice from electricians and kiln specialists or 'kiln doctors'.

www.jo-davies.com

Pouring Bowl by Jo Davies.

CHAPTER 1

WHAT IS A KILN FIRING?

Kiln firings is the area of ceramics that all ceramicists have in common. It is a leveller, an area of expertise, nuance, radical approaches and common ground. A ceramicist cannot exist without their kiln or some way of heating their work to a high enough temperature so that the clay they have shaped into existence turns into a hardened ceramic. However, there are some exceptions to this, and I feel it is important to mention artists like Phoebe Cummings, who makes her work with care and attention but then actively encourages it to dis-integrate, either with the use of dripping water or by other means, to beautiful effect. However, clay is, for the vast majority of time, dependent on kiln firings to be made permanent and finished.

For clay to become ceramic it must be heated, or fired, to above 700°C. Although each clay has a slight variation on this and firing this low would result in a very soft, brittle ceramic, this is the temperature at which it changes, at a molecular level, from clay into ceramic. All kiln firings work on the given that 'everything has a melting point' and we are working up to, and sometimes beyond, this point for our chosen materials. Having a knowledge of how our chosen materials will behave at different temper-atures is key to developing the kiln firings we use. Thankfully much of the heavy lifting of this has been done for us across generations of ceramic cultural

Kiln controller at Katharina Klug's studio.

development so the designed, constructed clays we most often use now will give some insight into this information before we begin to work with them.

A kiln is any form of insulated chamber that will allow heat to rise inside it. This can be a permanent structure made from non-flammable materials like brick or stone, or it can be a thickly made structure made from flammable materials like wood. Its walls could also be formed from a simple earth pit or a structure made from engineered firebricks which are either encased for permanence by metal or built and then un-built after each firing for impermanence

Coral Vases by Jo Davies. High-fired, stained porcelain with black manganese glaze and 24ct goldleaf.

and flexibility of scale. The different approaches to kilns around the world are many. Cultural differences in kiln technology are visible in the objects that are made by each culture because their tools will reflect the values, tastes and preferences of each indigenous population. Ceramics is no different and, in some ways, through its relative longevity, the field of ceramics is a prime candidate for both a whimsical and utilitarian display of evolving culture.

A kiln firing forces all objects contained within it to change through a rise in the kiln chamber's atmospheric temperature to a maximum point. There is then a gradual cooling of the chamber, along with the cooling of the items inside it, after its top temperature is achieved. A firing is often referred to by its top temperature, for example a 1,260°C or 1,080°C firing.

The top temperature is set depending on the requirements of the materials inside the kiln, what they can withstand and the fuel used to fire the kiln. Within this book I will be making reference only to the composite ceramic materials contained within clay, glaze, slips, enamels and lustres that can be fired within kilns fuelled by electrically heated elements. Historically, wood was the original fuel source for kiln firings (later on, gas and electric joined it as cleaner, more easily controlled fuels) but here we will concentrate on the electric kiln as it is now the most commonly used kiln-type for firing clay objects.

The rise in temperature changes the molecular structure of the materials inside the kiln chamber to harden them and give them a greater permanence. The temperatures used take ceramic materials to the point, or just before the point, of melting. This is in order to force the fusing together of particles within the object. However, not all materials are compatible (issues most commonly occurring at the juncture between clay and glaze) so this is not always a straightforward process. Time must be taken to test the combination of materials and for trial and error. Sometimes these experiments will lead

to the unexpected and beautiful, and sometimes to disaster …

Throughout this book I will also use examples of ceramicists who use well-known techniques in combination with innovative, or simply unusual, kiln practices in order to gain uniquely interesting results. I will do this to illustrate that the use of conventional practice as a springboard to development is necessary in order to push innovation forward and achieve our creative intentions. There should always be some room for the stretching of rules in any practice.

THE GENERAL STORY ARC OF A CERAMIC KILN FIRING

1. Bone-dry clay or ceramic with glaze or overglaze loaded into the kiln
2. Evaporation of any remaining water and extraction of gases from the clay body as the kiln heats
3. Clay fully dry and starting to change its molecular structure by 600°C
4. Molecular fusing of clay particles above 6–800°C and turning from clay into ceramic
5. As the heat rises the ceramic particles continue fusing together causing the shrinkage of its body
6. Top temperature of the kiln firing, as preset by the ceramicist loading the kiln, is reached
7. The ceramic may or may not sit at the top temperature for a preset duration (a 'soak' or 'dwell')
8. Kiln cools naturally

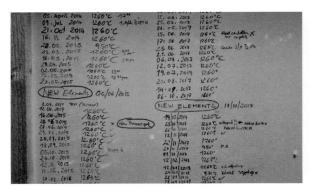

Katharina Klug firings.

THE MEANING OF 'EARTHENWARE' AND 'STONEWARE'

When the words 'earthenware' or 'stoneware' are used in ceramics it is, at a basic level, a reference to the upper kiln-temperature limits of either a clay, glaze or slip – most ceramic materials can be divided into these two categories and are often prefixed by either word, for example an 'earthenware glaze', a 'stoneware clay', and so on. They refer to one of two kiln temperature ranges:

- Earthenware clays/glazes withstand firing temperatures up to 1,200°C
- Stoneware clay/glazes withstand firing temperatures up to 1,300°C

These terms give an indication of the temperature range in which, for example, a glaze will melt and be at its best or where a slip will be at its most colourful. On the other side of this coin, it is also a caution telling us that, for example, if an earthenware clay is fired to the higher stoneware temperature (that is, above its upper limit of 1,200°C) then it will lose its structural integrity, slump or even melt.

'Earthenware' refers to any ceramic material's ability to withstand kiln temperatures of up to 1,180/1,200°C and 'stoneware' refers to materials that can withstand kiln temperatures above 1,200°C, but usually only up to 1,300°C. Most modern clays, glazes, slips, raw materials – particularly in Western ceramic culture – have been designed to fall within these brackets. Above all, it is important to take into account these factors when considering the compatible combinations of those materials. This is not to say that only earthenware clay plus earthenware glaze, or stoneware clay plus stoneware glaze, can go together but taking their compatibility into account can make things easier.

If firing earthenware above 1,200°C there is a risk of the clay slumping and melting; the same is true of stoneware clays above 1,300°C. Of course, the words earthenware and stoneware carry with them all sorts of other meanings around the look and feel of a ceramic object, such as its colouring and its durability; stoneware clay is considered more durable whereas earthenware clay is often mainly used for domestic ware and would not normally be left outside to endure the weather like its stoneware counterparts. The earthenware temperature range also has a reputation for being more colourful than materials in the stoneware temperature range, which traditionally has been known for its more muted colours, partly because the high kiln temperature can burn out the colour contained in glazes and slips firing to stoneware. That said, ceramic technology has moved on in recent years with many excellent, industrially produced stoneware stains that can be added to base glazes/slips to produce vibrant colour even at high stoneware temperatures, so the reputation for muted colour is falling away. However, it should also be considered that stoneware temperatures bring more risk of firing faults, are harder on the life of a kiln and are less economical and ecological. If we can find clays and glazes that achieve similar results with equal durability – or at least durability for our intended purposes – should we actually be considering the earthenware range as a viable option more frequently than we currently do?

When we first begin to work with clay we most often start by just thinking about the clay, and thought for the surface is delayed or even avoided. Finding the surface finish for the pot/sculpture/ jewellery/installation we have spent so much time on is daunting but you can mitigate this by choosing to start with the surface of your object. By this I mean before you have spent the time perfecting the clay part of your work, choose your glaze/slip/ gilded finish/and so on. Whether this is a bought-in glaze or studio-developed from raw materials, it can be hugely beneficial to work this way because the technical path to finishing your work will be clearer; this is because once you know this then the type of firings to use, the glaze firing temperature and which clay is best for the intended object will all be much clearer. For instance, the clarity of colour will be partially dependent on the clay that lies beneath it – an iron-rich stoneware clay may not be the best option if a glassy, pale green celadon is the goal as the two will interact, with colour from each material leaching from one into the other and creating a murky finish.

Once your combination of materials is chosen you can determine your kiln schedule. In the West we tend to bisq/bisque/biscuit our greenware (unfired clay) before glazing them and returning them to the kiln for a second firing. Other cultures often 'single-' or 'once-' fire items with glaze already on the greenware for a single firing.

The reason for bisq firing is in order to ensure we have a stable, durable ceramic surface before applying a glaze. It also limits damage to the kiln as explosions and collapses are more likely when firing greenware – if these occurred with glaze present then the damage would be much more extensive because molten glaze on kiln shelves, elements and thermocouples becomes a much more costly mistake than the comparatively 'dry' dust and rubble of a standard bisq-kiln blow-out which contains no glazed items. Single-firing also requires both glaze and clay to have the same temperature range so separating the two allows a wider scope of possibilities. Also, historically speaking, the introduction of bisq firing reflects the early days of a surge in development in the European ceramic industry inspired by the arrival of Chinese porcelain in the 1600s (*see more on this below*). For quite some time the failure rate of kiln firings was so high that, for the reasons outlined above, bisq firing was introduced.

BISQ FIRING

A bisq firing (also known as bisque or biscuit) is the firing used to turn clay into hardened ceramic but without any glaze. This is the first firing, after which glaze is applied to the ceramic and returned to the kiln for its second glaze firing. In the UK bisq firing, as a concept, came with industrial developments in Stoke-on-Trent but other parts of the world have a history of dividing bisq and glaze firings well ahead of this. The development of the clay we now know as bone china was inspired by the import of Chinese porcelain into Europe, starting in the late sixteenth century. Prior to this, British ceramic culture had been a smaller industry with the use of earthenware clays being prevalent and the colour being mainly in the iron-oxide range – browns, yellows, creams – and was very much a cottage industry. The popularity of the jade-like Chinese celadon, bright white and cobalt blue objects being produced during China's Ming Dynasty spurred a search across Europe, including Britain, to create similar ware. The Staffordshire potteries developed their own methods to create what became known as English porcelain but the recipes and methods were very different to the ones used for Chinese porcelain – which is a predominantly naturally occurring clay, fired in wood-fired kilns at that time and, more commonly, in gas-fired kilns now. The Chinese firing method was all or nothing, with clay and glaze being fired once; the extra bisq firing of the British potteries would have struck the Chinese as wasteful in the extreme and many Chinese factories and potters still once-fire porcelain as a matter of course to this day. However, in British factories at the time a separate bisq firing became a necessity because of inherent unreliability in the new materials being used; bisq firing's place in ceramic culture remains the dominant way of working today.

In short, a bisq is the first firing of your clay, without any glazed surfaces, which will give you a reliable and porous surface on which you can apply glaze or slips if you choose to. The bisq also gives us an opportunity to see which items are viable before investing any more time and materials into them. If an item cracks or warps we can choose to discard it after the bisq firing.

Low- or High-Bisq Firing?

We usually choose between two types of bisq firing – low bisq to 1,000°C or high bisq to 1,140°C. I have noticed anecdotally that high bisq is starting to be used less and less but it remains useful if we understand the reasons behind bisq firing.

Bisq firing temperature is determined by several factors. Working backwards in the process, the first factor is the temperature range of the glaze we intend to use, the second is the temperature tolerances of your clay and the third is the creative intentions of the maker. Within these parameters there are several broad brushstroke issues to consider. These broad issues can then be paired with the individual, detailed refinements of the process that each individual maker develops according to their creative intentions.

The key superficial difference between high and low bisq is the top temperature – 1,000°C for a low bisq and 1,140°C for a high bisq. Clay hardens, and becomes less porous and more dense, the higher the temperature it reaches in the kiln. A clay that has fired to 1,000°C will be more porous than the same clay fired to 1,140°C. This is key in terms of glaze adhesion onto the ceramic surface at both the application stage (whether you are dipping and pouring the glaze, spraying or brushing) as well as within the kiln firing itself, when it will bind to the surface. If we think of the pores of the ceramic surface as a 'key' for glaze then this can help to illustrate how glaze and ceramic bind together. If a ceramic has larger pores for glaze adhesion then it can be easier to apply the glaze and can result in a thicker layer of glaze. Conversely, a ceramic with small pores can mean a layer of glaze that is too thin.

In terms of the clay body, best practice says that we should fire our clay high enough in temperature in order to mature it to a point where it is hardened and durable. This can happen during either its bisq *or* its glaze firing. The clay body will harden and become less porous the higher it goes in temperature so, for instance, firing a stoneware clay in a low bisq (1,000°C) and then returning it to the kiln with a low-firing glaze to around 1,020°C does not take stoneware ceramic into as durable a state as it could be. This is because a stoneware clay, by its nature, withstands temperatures between 1,200°C and 1,300°C so the closer we can get the stoneware clay body to this the better. In this example, a better solution would be to either fire the ceramic in a high bisq of 1,140°C before the glaze firing at 1,020°C or, better still, to change the glaze to a stoneware glaze allowing us to low bisq at 1,000°C and then return the item for its glaze firing that will be above 1200°C. When using a low-firing earthenware glaze with a stoneware clay, the high bisq is a compromise that gives the clay greater durability but still leaves it porous enough to accept glaze. However, I caveat this by saying this is a general rule and combinations of clay and glaze should always be tested for compatibility.

If wishing to use a glaze with a top temperature of 1,150°C or above on a stoneware body then a low bisq will be fine as the clay body will mature during its glaze firing.

In the high-bisq example above, allowing the clay to mature at a high-bisq temperature meant that it hardened but maintained enough porosity for the glaze to form an even and reasonable thickness across its surface. All clays have slightly different tolerances so checking or testing the firing ranges, including vitrification points, of the clay we are using will be an important piece of evidence in working out the best combination of firings. Testing different combinations is very important to the development process so we should leave time for this as the combination of clay, glaze, kiln and ceramicist is always utterly unique. The ceramic items we test should not be ones that we are afraid to lose so making sure there are plenty of reject pots, maquettes or test tiles available for this is vital to a thriving practice. However, one of the biggest factors in deciding your bisq temperature is in the glaze adhesion and therefore colour and texture response of the glaze as a direct result of the surface porosity of the ceramic.

Stoneware clay + stoneware glaze = yes
Low bisq then stoneware glaze firing

Stoneware clay + earthenware glaze = yes
High bisq then earthenware glaze firing

Earthenware clay + earthenware glaze = yes
High or low bisq then earthenware glaze firing

Earthenware clay + stoneware glaze = no (with very few exceptions to be discussed below)
Low bisq then low stoneware glaze firing of no more than 1,200°C

The final example above is for the most part not suitable because most stoneware glazes will only be best at a temperature that is higher than the earthenware clay's maximum temperature. If this combination is attempted, the clay will slump or even melt when fired to most stoneware glazes' ideal temperature. However, the exception to this rule is when you have a very low-firing stoneware glaze that vitrifies around 1,200°C – a top temperature which most earthenware clays will tolerate but some may be so close to vitrification themselves at this point that they may lose their shape; for this reason, test the exact combination of materials ahead of committing to this on anything precious. This combination may be a good candidate for single-firing (see description of single-firing later in this chapter).

Having tested the above combinations of bisq and glaze firings we may feel that we want to tweak temperatures to, for instance, increase or decrease glaze adhesion when we are dipping/spraying/brushing it onto the ceramic, or we might want to increase fluxing of the glaze in the firing, or even mitigate against a firing fault. In the consideration of adjustments like these we need to examine our

creative intentions as these will dictate the potential trade-offs we may need to make between technical issues and creativity. All these factors will be discussed further throughout the book.

In my own practice I have found that the Audrey Blackman porcelain I use won't accept glaze easily once it has been fired to high bisq so I will always fire to 1,000°C low bisq before glazing and returning the ware to the kiln for its glaze firing to 1,240–1,260°C. As a fine-particle, smooth clay, the very dense closing of its pores is inevitable but most stoneware clays contain a variety of sized particles giving them more tolerance and porosity and less overall density. A grogged stoneware will remain much more porous at high bisq than a smooth clay-like porcelain or bone china.

As mentioned, firing your clay too high before applying the glaze can create problems in glaze application but may also result in various issues with the glaze in its firing. It is possible that the glaze could 'slide off' the ceramic during its firing because of it not being keyed into the surface enough. The effect of a less porous, dense ceramic body can result in a glaze not adhering to its surface easily and the glaze appearing thin and/or lacking in colour. In short, we are looking for the correct porosity of ceramic plus the correct thickness of glaze according to our intentions.

This is because a more porous ceramic sucks the glaze onto its surface more readily, which can result in a thicker application giving the glaze a more 'full' look. However, glaze that is thickly applied may also make the glaze begin to flow, resulting in a dripping effect as the weight/volume of glaze on the surface makes it flow (or 'flux') with the rise in temperature of the kiln. Overly thickly applied glaze can also result in glaze crawling so conventional approaches would see this as a fault in the surface (see more on glaze crawling in Chapter 5).

Of course, if our intentions are to harness either of these effects within our ceramic objects then the concept of it being a fault is very much in

SEGMENTS OF A KILN PROGRAMME OR SCHEDULE

First ramp – This is the rate at which your firing will rise in temperature to start with. it is usually measured in degrees per hour.

First dwell/soak time – Soak and dwell are interchangeable terms and refer to the point at which a kiln firing holds a set temperature for a set period of time.

Second ramp – This is the rate at which your firing will rise in temperature for the second part of the firing. Most ceramic kiln controllers have two ramps but it is possible to find controllers with more. Measured in degrees per hour.

Top temperature – This is the maximum temperature that you wish your firing to rise to.

Final dwell/soak time – This is the amount of time the kiln will stay at the top temperature before cooling.

This Firemaster kiln controller shows a diagrammatic version of the rise, plateau and cooling of temperature during a kiln firing.

question. In fact, many ceramicists will use what might be considered traditional firing faults to great effect. Sculptural work tends to have more leeway in this because a matured ceramic body coupled with a glaze that has its structural integrity is of greater practical importance in functional items, so intention is very much everything. However, the historical ideas around what constitutes a firing fault is rooted in the development and production of functional ware because of the practical requirements of this type of ceramic object, but as soon as an object has no function then our conception of a 'fault' should be re-evaluated. When viewing ceramic sculpture, my own view is that disregarding objects simply on the basis that they have X or Y 'fault' feels very wrong and we should all caution against this. In part because it forces us to bypass the conceptual or emotional relevance of the work, which is where its value lies.

These two sample firing schedules, which are relatively cautious for hand-built or wheel-thrown items, allow for heatwork in the kiln to take place. 'Heatwork' is a term used to describe the effect of heat on ceramic materials plus time. In the bisq firing one of the results of heatwork is for the clay body to gain an evenly porous ceramic throughout and not just superficially. If your bisq firing is too fast you risk the heatwork being very superficial, that is, the outer layer of your ceramic will have a different porosity than the core because the heat has not 'worked' on it and the core has reached a lower

EXAMPLE BISQ-FIRING SCHEDULES

Low-bisq firing:
First ramp – 80°C p/h to 600°C
No dwell/soak
Second ramp – 100°C p/h to top temperature 1,000°C
Soak/dwell 10–15 minutes
Length of firing 11.5 hours

High-bisq firing:
First ramp – 80°C p/h to 600°C
No dwell/soak
Second ramp – 100°C p/h to top temperature 1,140°C
Soak/dwell 10–15 minutes
Length of firing 12.7 hours

temperature than the outer skin. This is of greater importance for hand-built or substantially thicker pieces, and very thin ware can have a speedier bisq firing.

Taking this into account, it is common practice in the utility-ware (bathroom/kitchen items) factories of Stoke-on-Trent to use a relatively long dwell/soak of an hour or more at the top temperature of the bisq firing to make sure the heatwork is completed on the thickly made items they are producing, as these items need to be robust because of their function. This is just one example of a strong reason for a comparatively long bisq firing with a view to fully stabilizing the ceramic body.

In ceramics we often talk about items 'twisting', which means a piece is effectively in a state of tension, slowly moving, because it has differing density levels running through it. This is of particular importance when it comes to the glaze on a piece's surface as this molecular 'twisting' can be reflected in the glaze through very visible crazing (*see* more on crazing in Chapter 5). This is another reason for a stabilizing bisq firing with opportunity for enough heatwork on the ceramic. The twisting can be so slow sometimes that crazing can appear years after the item has been removed from the kiln. If you are having trouble with unwanted crazing this can sometimes be resolved by increasing the soak time at bisq in order to create a more even body that is not twisting against the glaze and causing uneven surface cracking. I hasten to add that this is just one possible reason of several for a glaze to craze.

As mentioned, it is possible to speed up the bisq firing a little for very thin ware. However, the first few hours of your bisq firing play a big role in evaporating out the very last molecules of water from the clay. This should therefore still be done relatively slowly with the kiln vents left open for evaporation, and the release of gases, in the first part of the firing and then closed at around 600°C.

The explosive blow-outs inside kilns that ceramics is famous for are most often created by excess water inside the clay body evaporating very fast and the pressure of the steam escaping from the clay breaking it apart. This is why it is important for the clay to be completely dry before being fired. Significant air bubbles can also cause explosions because, as the clay shrinks with the heat of the kiln, the size of the cavities themselves become too small for the air contained within them and so the ceramic is blown apart in a similar way. However, the most spectacular blow-outs I have seen over the years have all been from excess water, which is, unfortunately, a mistake that even the most professional potters can continue to make long into their careers through impatience and looming deadlines. The danger of air bubbles in clay is often overstated and can be easily overcome by using clay straight from the bag or well-wedged clay coupled with a slow bisq firing similar to the above examples. However, you must handle your work in order to test if it is dry enough to be put into its first firing. Understanding what this feels like is a very important skill to acquire and only comes with practice.

If your clay is drying in a space with ordinary room temperature but feels cold to the touch then it is still too wet to go into the kiln. If your work is taking a long time to dry then consider the temperature and ventilation of the room in which it is being left to dry: if there is no airflow and the humidity is high then your work may take weeks to dry. Nothing beats a dry, sunny day outdoors to dry out clay for its firing. However, some clay or certain shapes will not tolerate the speed of this type of drying so slow-drying can be one way to prevent cracking, particularly for items made from component parts.

WHICH GLAZE?

Start with the glaze and work backwards. I agree that starting with the glaze ahead of all making, or even while still working with the clay, is not always possible or realistic. This is because the enthusiasm to simply make something from clay is often more important than what can feel like banal technical requirements determined by the restriction of materials and kilns. In the early days of a ceramic practice, musing over what glaze to use with, for instance, a myriad of wheel-thrown pots recently finished is a common situation. The glaze can become an afterthought. However, as a practice matures, it is possible to put the glaze joint-first in the development of a new project, at the very least by broadly considering if you would like to use a stoneware or earthenware glaze.

Your glaze's top temperature will either be in the stoneware range (1,200–1,300°C) or the earthenware range (up to 1,200°C). Very often a glaze will have a temperature 'range' of, for instance, 1,240–1,260°C (this would be a stoneware glaze) rather than a single top-temperature point of, for instance, 1,280°C on the nose. The temperature range indicates the temperature tolerance of our glaze and is where it will vitrify, which is when all the particles will be fully fused together. The variety of glazes available, either off-the-shelf products or ones developed from raw materials, is so wide that general advice on this is difficult to provide in a book with particular focus on the kiln. However, when embarking on a new project it is important to weigh up your creative intentions in terms of colour and texture against the requirements of function or sculptural intentions of the pieces being made. For example, does the item you are making need to be easily cleaned so it needs a glassy, easily sanitized surface or does this not matter for a sculptural piece being made? Narrowing the glaze possibilities for each project at an early stage will help us to decipher what is important in our glaze choice and therefore what can be ruled in

Glazed vessels at Akiko Hirai's studio.

and what can be ruled out as possibilities. As this book is working from the perspective of kiln firings, in this instance our main concern is with the glaze's temperature range (its vitrification point or top temperature), so once we know this we will have a clearer technical path.

The testing of the combination of clay, glaze and kiln is vital in the early stages of working out the glaze for a project. Try to avoid putting an untested glaze onto a 'final' object as there will, unfortunately, usually be a discrepancy between the actual outcome and the visualized intention. Using small test tiles – or better still, test pieces of a similar shape, made in a similar way to our final items – to check the viability of our glaze is always the best course of action. Ceramic objects take time to develop so it is important not to allow yourself to be hurried, or be in a hurry, for these results. From experience I have learnt that it can be a vital stitch in time to allow more time than first assumed to work out technical issues. This can even mean helping clients to understand the length of time it takes to develop new work and that a two-week deadline, for instance, is not enough for the best results.

The use of small test pieces that are very similar to our final objects – in terms of the process used to make them, clay used and shape – is best for ascertaining the appropriateness of a combination of clay and glaze as they are more likely to be a true reflection of outcome. This is because a change in clay, shape and texture, kiln, ceramicist and mode of production can give different results than expected. A change of kiln often results in a change of glaze outcome so testing an old glaze in a new kiln should be one of the first jobs if wishing to continue to use it in the same way. For instance, a recent change of kiln at my studio meant some adjustments to the firing schedule that had worked very well in my previous kiln.

Once you have an idea of surface finish it does make the technical requirements of the project as a whole more straightforward.

NO GLAZE?

In terms of deciding on your firings, using no glaze at all is of equal importance to using glaze. In the times when we would decide not to glaze the surface of our work, just one firing could be enough. For instance, some clays have beautiful surface finishes at higher temperatures – red earthenware terracotta becomes a very dense chocolate colour at around 1,160–1,180°C and porcelain can achieve

Sasha Wardell's bone china is often unglazed but high-fired, showing a preference for using body stains, or simply the clay itself, for colour.

a marble-like surface in its upper firing range of around 1,260–1,300°C. We may also have added a 'body stain' to a clay in order to colour it, which we may want to see without glaze for a more satin or matt finish. Some body stains even have a slight self-glazing effect because they act as both a colourant and a flux. When using body stains the firing temperatures should be tested according to the clay and tolerance of the stain being used – bear in mind that many body stains will lower the vitrification point of the clay they have been added to. For all these examples it is possible to simply fire from raw clay to a top temperature in one firing for a finished piece.

For any of these above examples, however, it is possible that there may be instances when a first, low bisq and then a second, higher firing would be necessary. This is because you may feel that sanding the surface with diamond pads to refine the surface finish will improve the look and feel of the object. This can be done more easily after a low-bisq firing of 1,000 which will give us a robust but slightly soft ceramic, firing a little lower will leave the ceramic even softer. Once this has been done the item can be returned to the kiln for a higher-temperature firing that will vitrify the ceramic body. This is because grinding/sanding the surface of any ceramic once it has vitrified is very hard work indeed so grinding it when the clay has turned to ceramic, and so has a suitable resistance but is not so hard as to be impossible to sand/grind easily. If sanding ceramics after a bisq, we can use 'wet and dry' sandpaper for sanding with water, which will remove the dust safely. However, bear in mind that standard wet and dry sandpaper may discard small black particles into the pores of the ceramic, which can remain even after washing the item; I have seen these end up fired permanently onto the surface when the item is returned to the kiln for its second firing. This is less of a problem with terracotta or a dark clay but much more of a problem with bright white porcelain. Diamond pads and cloths of all varieties are best for this and should always be used with water to take away dust – for both ease of use as well as for health. Please avoid sanding ceramic dry as it is extremely bad for health and creates a layer of dust in the studio that migrates everywhere. Even if choosing to sand outside or under air extraction, the repeated act of sitting over work while sanding could result in poor lung health down the line. The very simple measure of doing this with sandpaper or grinding tools designed to be used with water mitigates this issue well.

In addition, many clays burnish well, particularly terracotta and dark, smooth clays. This is done when the clay is at its leather-hard stage and before its bisq firing so, in this instance, just one firing is more likely to be all that is needed. See the work of Magdalene Odundo for beautiful examples of this type of burnished finish.

THE GLAZE FIRING

The function of a glaze firing is to vitrify or 'melt' your glaze onto the surface of the ceramic. The glaze firing usually rises in temperature faster than a bisq firing, particularly when compared to the first stages of a bisq, because the main heatwork of the glaze firing is happening at the upper temperatures when the glaze will be vitrifying.

As mentioned previously, glaze firing ranges fall into two categories – earthenware or stoneware. If using more than one glaze on an item it is common for all glazes used on this item to be either earthenware *or* stoneware. If using multiple glazes on one piece then there will need to be somewhere that all the glazes' firing temperatures overlap. For example, if one glaze has a firing range of 1,200–1,240°C and the other has a firing range of 1,220–1,260°C, a top temperature of between 1,220–1,240°C would be

appropriate as this would enable us to have just one glaze firing to accommodate both glazes, which makes economical and ecological sense.

Differing firing temperatures without any overlap can become difficult to manage. Although it is possible to separate out the required glaze temperatures into different kiln firings, starting with the highest first and working our way to the lowest temperature, this should be tested if results need to be re-created again and again as re-firing may have adverse effects on glazes already on the surface of the ceramic. For instance, one of my own glazes will not re-fire easily, turning milky and pitted if this is tried and especially if the ware has been sitting for more than a week after its firing.

On the other hand, the sculptor Tessa Eastman uses a combination of glazes in her work to beautiful effect, working very intuitively and sometimes deciding on further glaze additions only after having seen how the first glaze has come out – *see Tessa's Maker Profile for a fuller impression of her approach*. The parameters of a practice in terms of re-firing work is very much down to the volatility of the materials we are using so testing this can help to take away at least some of the jeopardy.

EXAMPLE GLAZE FIRING SCHEDULES

Stoneware glaze firing:
First ramp – 95°C p/h to 600°C
No dwell/soak
Second ramp – 130°C p/h to 1,260°C
Soak/dwell 10–15 minutes
Length of firing 11.4 hours

Earthenware glaze firing:
First ramp – 95°C p/h to 600°C
No dwell/soak
Second ramp – 130°C p/h to 1,080°C
Soak/dwell 10–15 minutes
Length of firing 10 hours

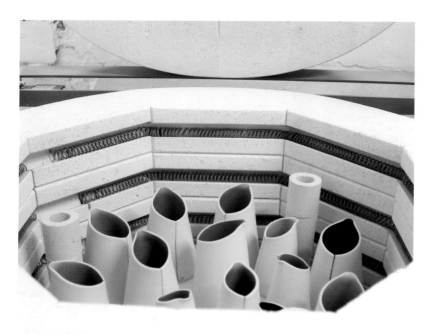

Jessica Thorn uses a combination of glazed and unglazed techniques creating bare porcelain outer surfaces in contrast with glazed, beautiful, functional interior surfaces.

Jessica Thorn tableware.

ONCE-FIRING OR SINGLE-FIRING

'Once-' or 'Single-Firing' are terms used to refer to a firing that combines both bisq and glaze, that is, when glaze is applied to raw clay and fired in one go. Many ceramic cultures around the world, such as porcelain producers in Jingdezhen, China, use this process whereas, in many Western cultures, the dividing of the firings has been used as a fail-safe against potentially sticky, molten, glaze-covered ceramic explosions. This is because the development of a sophisticated ceramic industry came later in European cultures (from the eighteenth century) when clay bodies were less reliably evolved than they are now; firing unglazed items first allowed for a certain amount of loss in the firing, without ruining kiln furniture or excessively wasting materials and time used in the firing and glazing. Ceramic cultures using single-firing habitually is a testimony to the reliability of materials as well as the highly developed skills of those areas.

In contemporary times the first bisq firing continues as an expected part of the process in Western cultures and would understandably be seen as a little wasteful by some others. However, the changing combination of clay, glaze and other materials in many small studios makes the risk of single-firing higher, although many ceramicists who are experienced with their formula of materials are very comfortable with the time- and energy-saving benefits of this method. However, the sensitivity to excess water in clay during firings should be established for a new clay, as this will be the main cause of explosions (*see* Chapter 5 regarding excess water). Items that are more thickly made tend to hold water well and are more likely to encounter firing issues of this kind, so once-firing items up to an average thickness is advisable.

Having established a compatible clay and glaze combination, your firing should be a hybrid of the two types of firing. As slow water evaporation is important in the early stages of a firing, the climb in

Bojo:Aliens by Annabel Faraday is an example of a single-fired piece. The use of partial glaze makes single-firing lower risk.

EXAMPLE SINGLE-FIRING

First ramp – 80°C p/h to 600°C
No dwell/soak
Second ramp – 120°C p/h to top temperature
Soak/dwell 20–40 minutes depending on thickness of
    items and glaze requirements

temperature should be no more than any other bisq. After 600°C the speed can be increased. It could be debated that the speed of the second part of the firing should remain the same as an ordinary bisq, with the top temperature landing within the vitrification range of both clay and glaze. An appropriate soak time for the heatwork on both the glaze and clay is advisable; this should allow the ceramic to be even as well as the glaze to be melted and vitrified. Of course, if a glaze cannot withstand a soak then perhaps single-firing is not appropriate in that instance. Generally speaking, glazes with a wider firing range for their top temperatures are better for single-firing as this suggests less volatility.

ENAMEL AND LUSTRE FIRINGS

Enamels have a wide range of colours that, unusually for the ceramic process, have a close likeness to the colour that can be expected after firing. Lustres tend to produce metallic or opalescent surfaces but look nothing like the final outcome so, as with so much ceramic practice, a leap of faith is once again required. Both enamels and lustres are also completely optional.

Enamels and lustres are two types of on-glaze – as this name suggests they are used as surface colouring that is painted/placed/sponged onto an already glazed and fired surface, and then re-fired in a third firing for enamel and fourth firing for lustre.

Enamels are the 'third firing' because their firings have a temperature range of around 8–850°C, taking place after the glaze and bisq firings, whereas lustres only fire between 7–740°C and are the fourth and final firing in descending order or temperature. These materials will burn out if fired too high so they are fired last.

Both enamel and lustre firings can be fired fast. In my own studio I tend to fire enamels and lustres at 150–170°C p/h all the way to the top temperature

---

EXAMPLE ENAMEL/LUSTRE FIRING

First ramp – 150–170°C p/h to 400°C
Dwell/soak – 30 minutes for a well-packed kiln
Second ramp – 250°C p/h to either *enamel 8–850°C* or *lustre 7–740°C*
Soak/dwell 10–15 minutes

---

required by each but a speedier second half of the firing can be programmed. If firing a lot of items, which will produce a lot of gases, a short soak time of thirty to sixty minutes at the midpoint of the firing, around 400°C, can be used to vent these gases from the kiln chamber. This will even out the kiln's atmosphere, ridding it of excess gas, which can interfere with the surface response to heat, before it continues to climb to the top temperature. Your kiln's digital programmer may not have the facility for a midpoint soak; if this is the case then consider slowing the whole firing slightly in order to vent the kiln throughout the course of the firing. A short soak of a few minutes to equalize the firing at the top temperature should be used but not for too long as this can burn out colours.

Officially, both enamel and lustre do 'better' on glossier glazes because the adhesion and colour response can be brighter but I have, for instance, seen some excellent use of gold lustre on bare, unglazed, high-fired porcelain – with the finish being more matt than the more usual high-shine surface that is synonymous with all lustres – so some experimentation is to be encouraged.

As a note on safety, venting gases away from a kiln during a lustre firing in particular is very important because lustre firings release toxic gases that are harmful to life, so please do make sure that your lustre kiln-firing is not venting into living or working spaces and/or that all extraction is being used during these firings.

DECAL OR TRANSFER FIRINGS

Decals, also known as 'transfers', give us the ability to place a printed image onto the surface of a ceramic. They can either be digitally printed or screen printed by hand but it is important to note that both transfers/decals are produced using enamel or lustre 'inks' so fire similarly to enamels and lustres, as described above. The image is printed onto a paper-like material that can then be manoeuvred onto the surface of glazed ceramic. Details on exactly how this is achieved can be found from the manufacturers of ceramic decals/transfers. However, the technology producing ceramic decals has developed to such an extent in the last twenty years that they are very inexpensive to have made in small or large quantities and so are a useful way to reproduce patterns and images on ceramic for anyone with access to a kiln.

As mentioned, once the decals have been attached to the ceramic, the firing schedules are similar to enamel or lustre firing schedules. However, all producers of decals, whether they are screen printed or digitally produced, have slightly different firing advice. I have found that the top temperature for this process is often marginally higher than ordinary enamel or lustre firings in order to fully burn out the paper. The manufacturer producing your materials will be able to give you the best advice on the kiln programme required but a fast ramp of around 180–300°C p/h to the top temperature is normally advisable. Some producers will advise a hold/soak in the middle of the firing in order to vent the kiln chamber of gases from cover-coats and other residual components used in their production, and a very short soak at the top temperature in order to burn away the transfer paper completely as well as even out the kiln's temperature for a good colour response. However, too long a soak, or too high a top temperature, can have the effect of burning out the colour so caution on this is best with regard to enamel surfaces of all kinds.

As with lustre firings, venting the atmosphere around the kiln is again of particular importance for decal firings because of the burning away of chemical components in the film/paper used for this process so please make sure your kiln is not venting into a living or working space without extraction.

A NOTE ON OXIDATION AND REDUCTION FIRINGS

Oxidation and reduction firings refer to the amount of oxygen inside the chamber of a kiln while a firing is taking place. Broadly speaking, an oxidation firing is a firing that includes, as the name suggests, oxygen in the atmosphere of the kiln whereas a reduction atmosphere is one where oxygen in the chamber of the kiln is reduced. Electric kilns generally work only as oxidation firings because the heating elements inside the chamber are simply heating the atmosphere by increasing electricity and therefore heat. However, both gas and wood firings are able to reduce the oxygen in the atmosphere of the kiln because they are fuel-burning and therefore oxygen-burning. For this reason, the amount of oxygen inside the kiln chamber can be controlled through the opening and closing of the kiln's vents and/or burners, thereby achieving a light or heavy reduction (very little, or a lot of, oxygen) which has big effects on glaze response. By using a fuel-burning kiln, ceramicists are able to control the level of reduction in order to achieve results that are very different to an oxygenated, electric-kiln atmosphere. For a start on achieving some level of reduction in an electric kiln please *see* 'Setters and Saggars' in Chapter 2 for some advice on a few ways to create burning atmospheres inside an electric kiln.

... intuition with the firing comes from repetition and experience.
— AKIKO HIRAI

Moonjar by Akiko Hirai.

Akiko Hirai is based at The Chocolate Factory N16 in East London. Her practice is anchored in wheel throwing but ventures into hand-building and altering her work, with a huge emphasis on surface development as a means of creating poetic surfaces that reek of value, substance and chaos. At the time of our interview, she has a large gas kiln and two much smaller top-loading electric kilns, which she uses in combination. Her electric kilns are used to bisq her work but also to re-fire glazed pieces whilst the gas kiln is used as a vehicle for the production of glazed surfaces.

The Chocolate Factory has been home to her first and only studio space since 2002 and its position in a highly multicultural inner city area informs her work as a ceramic artist. It is more usual for a ceramicist working with the materials she uses,

along with a large gas kiln, to be set in a rural area but this would be the antithesis of her drive, which she says would result in a lack of stimulation. One of the many reasons that Akiko remains at The Chocolate Factory is because of this balance of urban life with the ability to use the type of kiln she needs to use for her practice, which is an increasing rarity in built-up areas where cautious landlords and insurance companies seem to collude in a collective ignorance to prevent ceramic production. She has landed in a lucky situation.

The kiln pack I observed was for a gas reduction including several tall vases, bowls and a large vessel. She has a gas trolley kiln – meaning that the bottom shelf of the kiln is on wheels, allowing it to be rolled out, forward of the main kiln door – so that she is able to place heavier items easily onto the bottom

Akiko Hirai at her studio.

shelf before rolling it back into the kiln. Electric kilns are made in this way too so it is important to recognize their potential value in the studio.

This kiln is a recent acquisition because, as she says, 'we are not getting any younger' and the regular strain on the body and back when placing large pieces does not become easier. The trolley kiln in recent times has also allowed Akiko to glaze her large vessels *in situ*, negating the need to handle them to transfer them once decorated, which has the added benefit of no unnecessary disruptions to the delicate surface ahead of the firing. These surfaces are almost always made up of multiple layers – engobe, porcelain slip, glaze and even small to large shards of porcelain clay make up the surface of larger pieces – so the ability to not handle or lift these delicate pre-fired surfaces plays an important role in their preservation and the practicalities of the kiln aid this hugely.

Akiko will often re-fire her work to achieve desired effects and she will re-examine and re-glaze the surface before firing again. This second glaze firing will often be in the electric kiln because the

Terayama Teabowl by Akiko Hirai.

surface added will only need more heat rather than the starvation of oxygen (reduction firing) provided by a fuel-burning kiln. In ceramics the loss rate can be heartbreaking but a sign of a professional potter is that they are comfortable with this to a large extent, and Akiko is no different in this respect. However, this re-firing process is also hard on ware and can weaken it after several firings so she tells me that around half of all her large vessels and moon jars collapse in one of their multiple firings. This is par for the course and not a failure but a sign of her great endeavour and preparedness to push the material to its limit.

Prior to the installation of Akiko's gas kiln, her previous kiln was quite different, having been made up from firebricks and a steel frame, which she had made to order by a metalworker. The 'door' required rebuilding on each occasion she fired as it was made up of multiple, numbered firebricks and its efficiency/insulation was much lower than her current kiln. The internal walls of her studio were blackened by carbonization from the old gas kiln and its reduction was becoming less good due to the increase of carbon inside the kiln's atmosphere. It was eventually decided that a better kiln was needed, although the old, large kiln had stood her in good stead for many years, and with only a £2,000 initial investment. The new kiln allows, due to better efficiency and a cleaner reduction, a greater level of control through the use of up-to-date technology. She had previously had to babysit her highly manual kiln, often having to manage the reduction aspects of the firings in the early hours of the morning; now the kiln can be programmed and managed more easily with hours of sleep regained. In her own words she is more productive since being able to use the automation of the new kiln.

However, the experience of the very visceral process of the old kiln has informed her knowledge and is still put to use in the management of her new kiln. For instance, the ability to recognize and resolve problems in ceramics at all levels is important and, with this in mind, Akiko described to me times when, simply through a change in the smell of the kiln firing, she was aware that a burner had failed within it and was immediately able to rectify this. This story shows that the repetition of process has an under-the-skin effect on a ceramicist and this can only be built across years. A less experienced ceramicist may have lost the kiln load because of a lack of awareness at that point. If we spend time trying, repeating and learning then this will give us an ability, using all of our senses, to make our work – this knowledge is both intellectual and experiential.

As I was speaking to Akiko I was very struck by where, if anywhere, the line is drawn between creative intention before you begin development and the knowledge of the process that allows you to imagine how to develop creatively. Akiko was very clear that her work is about outcomes and not an all-consuming fascination with the process, as takes over some potters, but I wondered how the two could be disentangled after a certain amount of time. To me it appears that the process has become like any language for Akiko: a means of communication, to speak about inarticulate subject matter and manifest the outward expression of a gradual absorption of her surroundings.

Akiko's use of two electric top-loading kilns in combination with a large front-loading gas kiln is not uncommon. Many ceramicists specializing in gas firings now opt for a supplementary electric kiln because of its comparative energy efficiency. Plus the electric firing of greenware is less likely to produce carbon or excess gases within the firing and this allows for a 'cleaner' surface on which glazes and slips can be applied without their colour being contaminated by various particles.

The relative longevity of Akiko's tenancy at The Chocolate Factory has also allowed for a great deal of stability and development in her practice without the distraction of being moved on every few years, as has become the custom in that area of London by developers who move creative studios into empty buildings in order to fill the space and take an income before building lucrative residential space. The moving of a ceramics studio, with all its equipment, heavy materials, dust and assorted idiosyncrasies can become a huge interruption in the life of a ceramics studio which, I am sure, is why there are so many city potters with top-loading, easily moveable kilns rather than steady, heavy, long-lasting, front-loading ones.

Akiko's trolley kiln is easily accessible when pulled out.

Akiko is able to wheel the base of the kiln into the chamber.

The kiln chamber is rolled into place when small, lightweight pieces that may be less stable can be placed into the chamber.

CHAPTER 2

INSIDE THE KILN

Understanding the fundamentals of how to pack a kiln will help you to get the most out of your firings. Knowing what basic kiln furniture is available and the way it is used inside your kiln will build your understanding of how to maximize the efficiency of each firing because most kiln furniture is built to be constructed together with standardized dimensions that will allow you to stack and build your kiln pack. Having some knowledge of other helpful, off-the-shelf items that can aid kiln firings is also useful for enabling other unique projects that need special treatment in the kiln.

PACKING A KILN

The best results often come from a well-packed kiln. This is because a large number of items in a kiln will have an insulating effect which will help to heat the items inside the chamber as well as slow down the cooling process. This also provides better heatwork, which is essentially where the heat inside the kiln really penetrates the clay to turn it into an even ceramic or turns glaze from a powdered material to a melted surface.

Set up for one of Akiko Hirai's electric kilns at her studio.

Speak Crowd installation by Jo Davies at the Future of Craft Exhibition, London.

First layer of the kiln stack in Katharina Klug's front-loading kiln.

Second layer of the kiln stack.

The top layer of the kiln stack is now in place for this firing but the kiln stack can have as many layers as needed.

A kiln should be packed using kiln shelves held up with kiln props to maximize the number of items that can fit into the chamber. The props act as structural columns between each kiln shelf and come in a variety of sizes that can be stacked together or used as single props. The props should be placed in the same place on each kiln shelf in order to build structure into the kiln stack. There are differing schools of thought regarding the number of props per layer but, whether you use a prop in each corner or go for a three/six-prop configuration, it is important that your props follow a vertical line from the bottom to the top of the kiln pack. Props will usually be placed around the edges but, if you have a particularly large span, a central, supporting prop can be a good idea.

To start, separate items to be fired into similar heights – one height for one kiln shelf; smaller items can also be tucked in between larger items for best use of space but minimizing the height between kiln shelves will allow you to pack the kiln efficiently.

There should be a clearing of approximately 1–2cm above the top of the tallest item on one layer and the kiln shelf above as well as a gap of a similar scale between each item if it is a glaze kiln. Items being fired to bisq, with no glaze present, can be stacked together and in contact with one another for a well-packed firing. In my own bisq firings I will often fire enough ware in one bisq firing for two subsequent glaze firings. Leaving gaps between items is done in order to ensure the melting glaze does not fuse items together but these gaps should be sufficiently large to allow room for the glaze to expand with the heat of the kiln. Ceramic items will always shrink down to a smaller scale than they were in their original clay-state but it is important to remember that at the peak of the kiln's firing temperature a glaze can become voluminous, so a gap that is too small between pieces will be closed by the glaze and fuse items together.

Start by loading the shortest items first into the kiln. When starting to load the kiln it can be useful to have your kiln props in place to begin with and load your items around them. By beginning with the lowest items you are ensuring the kiln stack has a low centre of gravity. For instance, if starting with tall items at the bottom and many small items on kilns shelves above, you risk the stack being top heavy and the bottom layer buckling. For obvious reasons a collapsed kiln stack is not something we want.

In theory an increase in the heights of items placed on each subsequent layer can work but the tallest items may also be very heavy, so a judgement about this should be made. This is an example of where half-shelves can be used to good effect by allowing a tall or heavy item to be placed low down while the kiln stack is built to the side of it in the way described above. *See* Katharina Klug's Maker Profile for a good example of stacking around taller items.

When packing a front-loading kiln it is pretty clear to see when a kiln shelf will clear the top of an item but a top-loading kiln can sometimes be less clear when viewing from above. It can be useful to have a long, straight ruler or other flat item that can be balanced between two kiln props, and across

the item in question, to see if a kiln shelf will clear it. Another useful item in your arsenal can be a dentist's mirror to view less visible areas to check if glazed items are in contact.

A well-packed kiln will take longer to cool than a kiln with just one or two items in it. Slow cooling is often associated with more reliable results but knowledge of your clay and glaze combinations is vital for the best results for your intentions.

KILN SHELVES

Depending on the work you are making, how pristine your kiln shelves are can be more or less important. Some ceramicists need very flat shelves that remain relatively clear of glaze run-offs but some are able to use craggy kiln shelves for years and years without too much impact on their work. These preferences are down to the nature of your

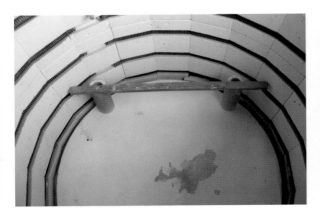

By balancing a straight stick across two props we can see if the kiln shelf will clear all the items on the lower shelf.

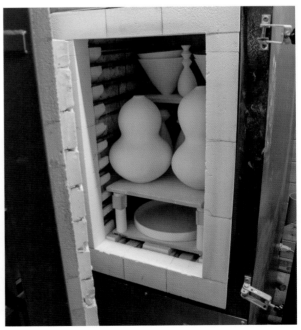

Here you can see that the stack does not always need to consist of complete layers; half-shelves can be used to accommodate work around tall items.

work. For instance, Akiko Hirai creates glazed surfaces that are highly controlled and considered but can also be volatile in the kiln. Working with this volatility results in beautiful work but exerts great pressure on much of her kiln furniture. However, when I interviewed her, I had the impression that the kiln had become almost seasoned with what some ceramicists, who make pale or white objects, would consider to be difficult-to-manage kiln contaminants but this has little to no bearing on her work.

Many kiln shelves will 'banana' after a lot of use so they may need replacing every now and then. In my own practice I need to replace shelves that do this because the bases of my ceramics need to remain flat; porcelain can sag at its top temperature thereby slumping into the shape it sits on. Whilst much of my work has an organic, curved quality, I do feel that rounded bases are not where this should be happening so the kiln shelves used for my work are replaced when warping begins to show in them.

Kiln shelves tend to last longer, when being fired to stoneware temperatures, if they are thicker – the wider they span, the more this is the case. You may decide to have thinner shelves if firing at lower temperatures or if you have a smaller kiln and need every last millimetre of space. However, there is also a trade-off in terms of the weight of thicker shelves against personal strength so the weight of the kiln shelves is something to think about if you struggle physically. For instance, back problems should be taken into account when considering shelf weight and size – this is the case if you have a top-loading or front-loading kiln. My personal experience of early back problems as an occupational hazard is that front-loading kilns are harder on the back if using weighty kiln shelves because a top-loading kiln at least allows gravity to help you when lowering them into the chamber. Having a mix of half-shelves and full-size shelves (for the size of your chamber) is good for reducing the need to lift a large weight every time.

KILN PROPS

A good selection of kiln props is vital in order to get the most out of each firing. They are used to build up 'layers' of kiln shelves within the chamber. Depending on the size and nature of your kiln you will need to work out the number of kiln props required per layer – this is usually three to six.

When working out the height of kiln prop to buy/use, consider the approximate size of items you are making when they are unfired and buy props that will clear this by approximately 5–10mm. For example, if you have three kiln shelves and decide to use three props per layer then you will need nine props of the same size. If you are making items that are a mixture of sizes then you will need props that are a mixture of sizes, in multiples of three, for this example. As your practice evolves you can add to this core equipment.

It is also a good idea to have a few kiln prop extenders in sets of three (again, if going on the example of three props per shelf, more if you need more props per layer) in order to raise the height

slightly of a layer and maximize capacity of the chamber. The reason for a good clearance between kiln shelves is because your glazes will expand with the heat of the kiln before contracting again when cooling, which could result in items nudging the shelf above leaving glaze on the underside of the shelf and the work unviable.

When packing a kiln I have found that it is best to start with the smallest items at the bottom of the kiln so that the shortest layer is at the base of the kiln stack. The reason for this is to keep the centre of gravity low in the stack and reduce the chances of it collapsing or moving. Very importantly, each prop should be placed on the shelf immediately above the one below so that a stable structure is created in the kiln with the pressure of weight from the shelves above being driven down through the props below and not creating uneven pressures across kiln shelves that may eventually result in your kiln shelves cracking and then snapping.

Kiln props can be bought in a range of heights.

PLATE RACKS AND TILE CRANKS

Plate racks and tile cranks can save space within the kiln by dedicating a much smaller area to multiple plates when not enough kiln shelves are available. Plate racks and tile cranks are inexpensive compared to kiln shelves and provide an efficiency of space compared to using many shelves for the same purpose. These items are fairly lightweight on their own but, when stacked up and fully loaded, can become extremely heavy with a lot of downward force onto the kiln shelf they are placed onto so, for this reason, situating these items onto the lowest shelf or, at the very least, onto a thicker shelf is advisable.

Plate racks and tile cranks can be used inside the kiln chamber to maximize the use of space. This type of kiln furniture comes in a variety of styles and sizes.

SETTERS AND SAGGARS

In the early days of industrial, large-scale production of ceramics it was common to use saggars. These are lidded containers made from fireclay and designed to hold the ceramic item inside the kiln in order to protect it from the ferocity of a fuel-burning kiln firing, which would have produced flame and uneven temperatures in large, cavernous wood-firing kilns. The theory is that the saggar would protect the ceramic from potential inconsistencies of heat,

carbonization and oxidation/reduction brought about by these types of firings, which would often be done on a very large scale using large bottle kilns (in Stoke-on-Trent) or anagama kilns (in South East Asian ceramic cultures). An electric kiln could be thought of as a way to re-create the pure heat atmosphere that a saggar provided through close insulation of the ceramic items in these large and difficult-to-control firings because the heat of each saggar becomes mainly atmospheric without flame coming directly into contact with the ware.

Paradoxically, in contemporary times, sometimes ceramicists will use saggars inside an electric kiln to create a small, controlled burning atmosphere immediately surrounding a piece using various combustibles like dry leaves, sawdust or even banana skins. Doing this will create different surfaces and potentially a glaze-like finish depending on which combustibles are used. For instance, ash glazes are so-called because wood ash is its base material; in a saggar firing using wood-based combustibles, it is possible to heat the ash to the point where it becomes glaze-like in one firing. Experimentation and open-ended expectations are required in this process.

Setters are related to saggars because, like saggars, they are used to 'set' a piece during a firing. Saggars, however, are lidded and often only follow the approximate shape of the pieces they hold; setters are closer to the negative shape of the base of a piece in order to help it maintain that shape during a firing and do not have lids. They can also be used to protect kiln shelves from the work or vice versa. For instance, some clays slump slightly within their vitrification range – porcelain is a prime example of this type of clay and its movement at this point is more likely if it is thinner. In my own practice I have occasionally made work that has round bases. These bases would have slumped and lost their shape, even if I did manage to make them stand inside the kiln, so it was necessary to create a bowl-like setter that

This small domed setter is used in my practice to allow for glaze. It was made by me at the studio and so is a bespoke solution to this particular problem rather than an off-the-shelf product. Most setters are made by the makers using them.

The lampshade is placed onto the domed setter. This is a bespoke setter made for this item but shows one of the many ways that this type of kiln furniture can be used. Like the lampshade that sits on it, the domed setter is made from porcelain to allow for shrinkage. Glaze is removed from the small area where the setter will be in contact with the lampshade during the firing.

followed the line of the curve of the piece in which to fire the work and mitigate this issue. Setters can also be used to raise an item up in order to prevent the glaze adhering to the kiln shelf.

Of course, sometimes it is possible to simply fire the work upside down on its rim, or other area that can be free of glaze and is flat. Porcelain, because of its shrinkage of around 20–25 per cent, requires the setter to be made fresh each time so the setter and piece being fired start and end at the same size. However, some clays which have much smaller shrinkage rates of around 5 per cent can have the same setter each time, made only slightly larger to accommodate the size of the pre-fired piece in conjunction with silica sand or alumina.

Flared Twist Pendant glazed and finished having been fired on a setter in the previous images.

SILICA SAND AND ALUMINA HYDRATE

Silica sand and alumina hydrate powder are used during a firing as an extra layer between clay objects and kiln furniture, usually shelves but sometimes setters. These powdered materials have very high melting points, well above the usual top temperature of 1,300°C, so do not melt even at the high stoneware range. They are multifunctional, acting as a layer on which clay can 'slide' as it shrinks, or to close a gap between the clay and a setter in order to maintain the shape of an unusual piece or between ceramic and kiln shelf as further protection from possible glaze run-offs. Silica is generally the coarser of the two materials and is often available in different grades. It is very good for larger pieces that may carry a lot of weight – the silica will facilitate their shrinkage by allowing them to slide more easily to their final, smaller size.

Alumina is normally milled to a very fine grade, much finer than silica, so is generally used for more detailed work or for clays that have higher shrinkage, like porcelain. The greater the shrinkage the greater the need to enable the sliding of the piece

although silica and alumina are certainly not always necessary. However, if your items catch on rough or bumpy kiln shelves they are more likely to warp. These materials are also useful for items that do not have flat bases that correspond easily to the flatness of a kiln shelf.

For instance, an undulating base may do well with sand or alumina underneath it: a pile of sand or silica would be placed on a kiln shelf (best done away from the kiln itself so excess silica/alumina is not spilled and full visibility can be had); then the piece is pressed into the powder to create a simple mould or negative of the item sitting on it, thereby giving the piece full support underneath and mitigating potential sagging during the firing. Alumina can be the better candidate for this type of use because it holds its shape better than silica due to its comparative fineness.

It is also worth noting that alumina hydrate is sometimes used as an ingredient to raise the melting point of a glaze and increase its mattness, opacity and durability. All because of its high melting point and colour. It is a good example of how one material can be used in ceramics to do very different things based on its melting point and context.

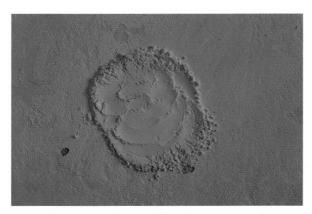

Alumina hydrate spread onto a kiln shelf ready for ceramic to be placed onto it during a firing.

KILN STILTS AND BEAD FIRING STANDS

Kiln stilts are useful for sculpture or functional ware that require a full wrap of glaze. Kiln stilts and bead firing stands are two ways to fire items that have a full wrap of glaze on the ceramic surface. Kiln stilts are multi-pronged, often star shaped, and designed to sit flat onto a kiln shelf with the ceramic item sitting on top. Stilts are either made from entirely refractory materials or are a combination of refractory materials and Kanthal-wire pins.

Whether using refractory stilts or stilts with pins, it should be made sure that the stilts can withstand the weight of the item they are 'stilting'. The stilts with Kanthal-wire pins are more expensive but last longer and can give better results because the Kanthal wire breaks away from the glazed area it has been in contact with more easily than their refractory cousins, leaving less 'scarring' on the piece. Both types of stilts usually require the use of a grinding stone to remove sharp glaze remnants from the piece where they were in contact. Glaze remnants can also be removed easily from Kanthal-wire pins using the same grinding stone used to remove sharp glaze from the ceramics. Doing this will help them to last longer and is part of good maintenance of equipment.

When using your grinding stone to remove or blunt sharp glaze left by stilts, wear eye protection as shards of glaze, even with a hand-held stone, often flick upwards into the face; gloves can also be a good idea to protect from sharp glaze after removal of the stilts.

Kiln stilts that are purely refractory (high-firing ceramic), with no wire props, can often end up embedded in glaze run-off or leaving more substantial scars on the glazed surface. If your items only require a thin layer of glaze that is relatively stable with little flow at its top temperature then these refractory stilts are up to the job. However, their pointed tips do become blunted quite quickly so they can only realistically be used a few times. This is reflected in the price difference between this variety and their metal-pinned cousins but, if you know you will only be stilting for a few projects, this saving may be worth it.

Bead firing stands are used to fire any item that has an unglazed, centralized hole. Ceramic 'beads' can be threaded onto Kanthal wire that is suspended between two points in order to allow for glaze around its entire circumference. This effectively allows the bead, or bead-like object, to be held in mid-air during a firing so the glaze can fully mature and melt without sticking to any surface within the kiln chamber. These items can be bought as an

Bead-firing stands can have Kanthal wire suspended between uprights in order for beads, or bead-like items, to be fired with glaze. The central hole should be free of glaze.

Kiln stilts made exclusively from a refractory material can last for just a few firings ('refractory stilts').

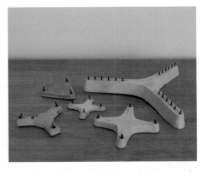

Kiln stilts with Kanthal-wire pins last much longer ('stilts with pins').

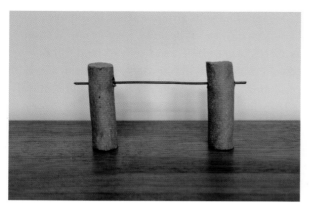

Studio-made bead rack with crank-clay pillars and Kanthal wire.

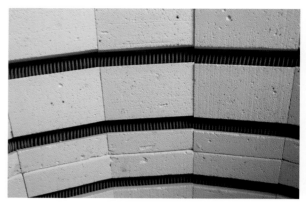

Kanthal-wire elements. In this kiln the elements are housed inside niches set into the brickwork of the kiln chamber. Some kiln designs have housing niches that are lined with refractory material (L&L Kilns commonly have this) or some even run elements along tubes that are set around the perimeter of the kiln chamber. These different approaches are designed to keep elements in place.

off-the-shelf product but the bead stand can also be made easily in the studio for more bespoke projects using two cones of fired crank clay with simple holes in each for the Kanthal wire, which can be easily bought from ceramic suppliers.

If trying this, bear in mind the weight of the items to be threaded as the span should not be too wide because the wire may sag heavily as the heat rises in the kiln; most Kanthal wire does not completely hold its shape, without support, above 1,200°C.

A NOTE ON KANTHAL WIRE

Kanthal wire is the most commonly used metal inside a kiln. This wire, at various gauges, is used as part of some kiln stilts and bead firing stands, as well as for the heating elements of the kiln. As Kanthal wire heats up it becomes more malleable and soft, particularly when going into the stoneware firing range (1,200–1,300°C), so its ability to hold its shape becomes impaired at these very high temperatures. Kanthal wire is used to create the coiled heating elements that work their way around the perimeter of a kiln and so, beyond 1,200°C, the housing niches for kiln elements really play their part in maintaining its shape even though the wire itself is often graded to temperatures between 1,300–1,340°C.

This softening of the Kanthal wire at high temperatures is the reason that most bead racks and metal-pinned stilts, which use Kanthal wire, are generally only used up to an absolute maximum of 1,200°C. The sagging of the wire beyond this point would work against the purpose of its use for obvious reasons and, very often, this sagging can happen a little earlier, between 1,100–1,200°C, for heavier items. Using Kanthal-wire-based kiln furniture is therefore often only encouraged within the earthenware firing range.

However, stainless steel versions of kiln stilts and bead racks are also now available and can withstand up to 1,250°C. This is important because it gives us the ability to use stoneware glaze between 1,200°C and 1,250°C in combination with these types of kiln furniture but caution regarding the weight of items is also advised as this can still cause stainless steel wire to sag at the upper limit of this temperature range. Testing any kiln furniture that uses Kanthal wire using unglazed items of a similar weight to the objects you intend to glaze, and taken to the same top temperature, will give you an idea of where this particular boundary lies.

THE ELEMENTS

As mentioned, the elements of an electric kiln are also made from Kanthal wire. One kiln usually has several elements, each one completing an electrical circuit from the power source, and housed in tight niches around the perimeter of the kiln. If an element has a loose connection, snaps or breaks down through age then this electrical circuit will not be complete and so a lack of heat on that element, and in the firing overall, will be the result. It can be difficult to identify this fault before having a misfiring kiln unless an element has clearly snapped and an obvious break is visible.

Most kilns will have a number of elements. Each element, depending on its position in the kiln, is set up to take a certain amount of electricity, and therefore heat, with some elements graded to become hotter than others. This design is to ensure that there is even heat throughout the kiln chamber but large discrepancies in atmospheric temperature between the top and bottom can indicate an issue with one or more elements.

The elements are one of a handful of kiln components that will need the most attention as they can be prone to sag out of place or snap, and will need replacing periodically just through wear and tear. Broadly speaking, regular stoneware firings will shorten the life of a set of elements whereas firing at earthenware will be easier on them. *See* Chapter 7 on kiln maintenance regarding maintenance of the elements where this will be discussed in more depth.

THERMOCOUPLES

Thermocouples are the heat sensors inside your kiln chamber that feed back temperature information to your kiln controller or read-out. Many electric kilns just have one thermocouple, which can be identified as a small, white ceramic prong sticking into the kiln. The thermocouple is usually a component to

The thermocouple can clearly be seen here as the white prong extending slightly into the kiln chamber. The brickwork around the thermocouple is made up of the lightweight firebrick most commonly used in contemporary kilns.

be checked periodically for cracks or breakages and care should be taken not to knock it with kiln shelves when loading the kiln chamber. No kiln furniture or items to be fired, even at bisq, should be in contact with the thermocouple and a good radius of space should be left around it so it can read an accurate atmospheric temperature without being 'influenced' by the heat of a kiln shelf, prop or ceramic item that will inevitably hold the heat differently to the atmosphere of the kiln.

KILN BRICKS

The bricks of a kiln are made up of refractory materials, usually within the suite of materials common within ceramics. They come in different varieties and so can be quite dense and heavy or more aerated and lightweight. The lightweight versions are more commonly used in ready-made electric kilns but the denser versions will often be used when a ceramicist is building a permanent, bespoke kiln-structure – this is more commonly done for fuel-burning kilns.

Lightweight kiln bricks or firebricks are more vulnerable because they are more powdery and soft so can be broken and damaged easily but, in theory at least, being encased within the metal chassis of a ready-made kiln, will be protected. These types of bricks are most vulnerable when a kiln is being moved so any potential twisting or excessive vibration of the kiln should be avoided. However, because they are so soft, the aerated bricks can be easily cut, scraped and scratched into bespoke kiln furniture when setters or props for lightweight work may be required. If doing this a dust mask should be worn as these bricks do also remain quite flaky, with dust and small debris coming away from them easily. It is for this reason that care should be taken when using these bricks inside the kiln chamber – because of dust deposits potentially dropping onto ceramic items within glaze firings.

THE SPYHOLES AND BUNGHOLE

There are always openings at the top and/or sides of an electric kiln. The side openings are 'spyholes' and the 'bunghole' is at the top of the kiln. Sometimes they are all referred to as bungholes but the opening at the top of the kiln is certainly never a spyhole – the heat pouring from it would make this impossible. A 'bung' is the name for the stopper used to cover or fill openings of this kind in a kiln. Larger electric kilns will often also have what is referred to as a 'damper' over a flue at the top, or sometimes the base, of the kiln. All these types of vents are doing similar things which is to create vents for gases.

Spyholes, as the name suggests, are for viewing the firing as it progresses, allowing us to view the kiln chamber, pyrometric cones and colour of the firing to gain an indication of the temperature – when the atmosphere is starting to turn from black to red, this tells us it is approaching 600°C with the orange hue deepening gradually as it rises.

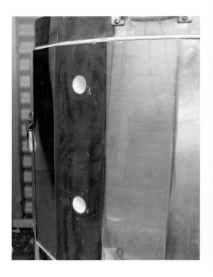

Spyholes in the side of a top-loading kiln.

Spyholes with bungs in place.

Pyrometric cones can also be carefully set up inside the kiln, with a clear line of sight from the spyhole aperture, to be watched as they bend and melt. *See more below about cones in Chapter 3.* Spyholes can have a dual use as venting holes but should be closed off using bungs over 600°C. The bungs can be taken out to observe cones but should be replaced once this check has been done. Make sure your bung is a neat fit for the sake of good insulation. The bunghole at the top of the kiln is normally left open for the first portion of the kiln firing in order

Bunghole and bung on the lid of a top-loading kiln. The bung is used to close the venting hole during a firing. Bungs like this are used to close spyholes of this variety too but there are many differing designs for opening/closing spyholes and venting holes in a kiln.

to allow the release of water vapour and gases that will be escaping the clay in the kiln – this is the case both for bisq and glaze firings. Standard practice is to close the top bunghole at, or just before, 600°C as this is when all water and the vast majority of gases have been extracted from the clay/ceramic. You may notice that your firings smell more strongly in the first half because of this.

Allowing all water to evaporate through the venting holes gives the kiln itself the best chance of a long life as the trapping of water vapour inside the chamber during a firing corrodes and rusts its components because water vapour is not cleared well. Rust can sometimes be seen around the metal of kiln doors and lids, which is often where water has been escaping during a firing so, in addition to leaving the bung open during the first portion of a firing, care with the maintenance of the ceramic fibre, or maintaining a good fit, around this area should be taken. Rust in these areas can result in unwanted iron oxide deposits inside the kiln chamber and on glazes.

If you have a front-loading kiln then a larger bunghole will be in place – usually at the top of the

kiln but sometimes at the base – with extra metal for levers or structure for the damper to be opened and closed. If this is the case then this area is a hotspot for rust and should be maintained frequently by hoovering the metalwork to rid it of loose rust. From experience, the position of these venting holes on front-loading kilns can make them harder to see and reach; they often have closing mechanisms that can easily deposit rust into the kiln chamber unless careful cleaning and maintenance are done.

Forgetting to close the bung at the right moment may not be the end of the world for your firing, particularly at bisq, but could result in rapid cooling or an uneven or under-fired (not reaching top temperature) kiln if the bung is not put in place at all. These issues are more of a problem with glaze firings which, although they are generally happy to have a faster rise in temperature during their firings, are less forgiving of rapid cooling, which could cause the shattering of glazed items in the worst-case scenario.

This attention to avoiding thermal shock should also be taken when you are ready to open the kiln after a firing. Spyholes and bungholes can be used to slightly speed up the cooling of a firing – starting with opening the smallest spyholes first, from about 350°C, and graduating to opening the larger bunghole at the top of the kiln as it cools further. Theoretically a bisq kiln can be 'cracked' – meaning the door is open slightly – at just below 300°C but this should only be done if under pressure and is not good for the elements. However, more caution should be taken with the opening of a glaze firing – natural, not forced, cooling to a low temperature below 100°C being the best option. The shattering of items in the kiln may not be a dramatic event but can also manifest as a hairline crack in the ware that annoyingly leaks water from the base of a cup or the crazing of the glaze shortly after the firing itself is finished and forgotten. As a rule of thumb, it should be taken that all materials prefer gradual, even cooling.

KATHARINA KLUG

Group of *Segment Moon Jars* by Katharina Klug.

Katharina is a potter specializing in wheel-thrown porcelain – her beautiful work is predominantly white and decorated with black linear patterns and some red. When I spoke to her in 2021 she was still at her garden studio in Cambridge, which she has since left to build a new workshop at a new home in the city. The old home studio, built around 2010, was light-filled and of a reasonable size of 30m² with windows facing the house and green spaces of the garden. It fell within the limits of 'permitted development' so no permission from the council's planning office was required for it,

although she did tell me that she sought approval from her neighbours ahead of embarking on the project, which seemed like a sensible move. She was originally prompted to build a home studio because of the restrictions on access and therefore ability to fire kilns overnight at rented studios. Plus, the flexibility of a space at home for a ceramicist is great as the ability to keep an eye on the evaporation of pots, or the rate of a kiln firing, is so much more convenient if switching between the responsibilities of home and work.

Jugs by Katharina Klug.

Studio detail.

From this studio Katharina ran two main electric kilns in a small kiln room inside the main space – these two kilns consisted of one front loader and one top loader. The older and now more decrepit front loader is a Heatworker from Potterycrafts. It is used for low-bisq firing and the newer Nabertherm top loader is her glaze kiln. There are several reasons she cites for attributing one kiln for bisq and one kiln for glaze, the main one being that some inaccuracy in a bisq firing is tolerable whereas greater temperature accuracy in a glaze firing is hugely preferable. The glaze firings are left to the newer Nabertherm top-loading kiln whilst the older Potterycrafts front-loading kiln takes the strain on bisq firings. The Heatworker, in Katharina's practice, was once the glaze kiln in its younger days, servicing

Katharina Klug's kiln room housing a front-loading kiln for bisq and a top-loading kiln for glaze firings.

1,260°C stoneware firings, but is now enjoying a retirement as a bisq kiln after a malfunction that made its temperature less reliably accurate. In time, the Nabertherm may have a similar retirement.

The other thing to mention in this type of setup is that the elements in an exclusively bisq-firing kiln will last for years as they will fire no more than 1,140°C (no more than 1,000°C in Katharina's case) so their degradation is demonstrably slower than elements firing to stoneware temperatures in excess of 1,220°C consistently. Slowing the degradation of elements is a good thing when stoneware firings are used regularly as these high temperatures really wear them out so if we can use a second kiln for the bisq this will help to do this.

Another reason is that it can also be useful to have a second kiln in times of 'emergency' when, if one goes down, the other can take up the slack if trying to meet a deadline.

Nabertherm, the brand that Katharina uses for her glaze kiln, currently has a good reputation for reasonably priced but high-quality kilns with great accuracy. Nabertherm grades their Kanthal elements for stoneware kilns at a slightly higher top temperature of 1,320/1,340°C than the usual 1,300°C that

some other manufacturers offer. As discussed in this book, the very highest that most clays and glazes need to reach is 1,280/1,300°C but the higher-temperature elements have a little more longevity. This is one of the things that made Nabertherm more attractive to Katharina because she consistently fires her porcelain to 1,260°C. Although this would be within the range of normal elements that are graded to 1,300°C, the higher-firing elements, due to the need for a high stoneware temperature every time it fires, will retain structural integrity more than their 1,300°C cousins, thereby holding their shape without softening as much as elements that would be on the edge of their limit.

This over-engineering can have the effect of preventing elements from sagging out of their housing and therefore potential malfunctions can be mitigated. Taking elements to their absolute limits each time we fire means they will need replacing more frequently so this innovation by Nabertherm is an interesting one. Katharina opted for a top loader but Nabertherm also offers an 'H' version in some of their front-loading ceramic kilns, which have Kanthal elements graded to 1,340°C. The benefit of this is giving even more longevity to the elements, especially if your practice requires soaks/dwells at stoneware of longer than ten to fifteen minutes.

Katharina's practice is interesting because she has a family history in ceramics. Her mother worked as a ceramicist with her business supporting a family of six through the 1980s and 1990s. The pottery was at Katharina's family home in Austria and her mother allowed her, with some help although not formally, to have a go in the studio. As a result she could throw a pot by the time she was ten, which is a highly impressive thing as the dexterity required to do this is usually only available to those who are more mature. Her studio, work ethic and creative intention show a deep understanding of the process in its entirety, which I believe is partly because of her strong familiarity with working in ceramics from an early age.

Low bisq:
60 p/h to 500°C
300 p/h to 1,000°C
No soak

Glaze firing:
200 p/h to 600°C
Full power to top temperature of either 1,255/1,260/1,265°C
Soak for 40 minutes

Katharina is loading glazed items into the top-loading kiln. The props are in place before starting to load.

The shortest items are at the lowest level in the kiln.

The next kiln shelf is put in place ready for the next layer of items.

The items to the right are of a similar height so a half-shelf can be placed across them thereby leaving room for taller items to the left.

The half-shelf is placed on the right once the shelf immediately below is full.

More items are placed according to their height.

The kiln is filled, with all pieces having a comfortable amount of space around them to accommodate their glaze. Glazed items should never be in contact during a kiln firing as they are liable to fuse together.

CHAPTER 3

RUNNING THE KILN FIRING AND SETTING THE FIRING PROGRAMME

Deciding how to manage a kiln firing is an important question. The answer to this can very much be dictated according to our confidence levels, time constraints and knowledge. We are able to manage kiln firings by manually turning them up or down, with the help of pyrometric cones, or by using a digital kiln programmer that can do this for us. A combination of both pyrometric cones and digital technology can also be used.

If purely using cones the kiln itself can be a very simple piece of equipment and these types of kilns can be very cheaply acquired. If using a digital kiln programmer to control the temperature of the kiln there is a wide variety of capability available, from a simple digital temperature read-out, which also requires us to turn up the kiln manually, to a fully programmable controller that orchestrates the climb in temperature, its soaks, top temperature and cooling. The last kind is now very common as the technology in this area is good but many studio-based ceramicists will use cones in combination with digital technology to, at the very least, occasionally test their kiln's temperature accuracy, with some doing this every time.

PYROMETRIC CONES

Pyrometric cones are small 'spikes' that are industrially made from refractory material. Each spike is labelled with a number and graded to melt at a specific temperature. The biggest brand of cones is Orton, which has a sliding scale of cones – for example Orton Cone 7 will melt at 1,240°C or Orton Cone 9 will melt at 1,280°C – showing the ceramicist a highly accurate indication of temperature, which can vary a little from the digital read-out and thermocouple gauging this.

> *Pyrometric cones deform due to the formation of glass and the pull of gravity as they are heated to their designed operating temperature. This is known as pyro plastic deformation. Careful control over the shape and composition allows Orton to provide a standardized product that reliably performs to known heating conditions. Cones bend and deform in an arc as they start to develop glass within.*
>
> ORTON LTD

Hanging Vases by Jo Davies.

Temperature equivalents (°C) for Orton Pyrometric Cones

	Self-supporting cones		Large regular cones	
Heating rate used	**60°C/hr**	**150°C/hr**	**60°C/hr**	**150°C/hr**
How fast was your firing rate	**Medium**	**Fast**	**Medium**	**Fast**
Cone number				
022	586	590	NA	NA
021	600	617	NA	NA
020	626	638	NA	NA
019	678	695	676	693
018	715	734	712	732
017	738	763	736	761
016	772	796	769	794
015	791	818	788	816
014	807	838	807	836
013	837	861	837	859
012	861	882	858	880
011	875	894	873	892
010	903	915	898	913
09	920	930	917	928
08	942	956	942	954
07	976	987	973	985
06	998	1013	995	1011
05½	1015	1025	1012	1023
05	1031	xxx	1030	1046
04	1063	xxx	1060	1070
03	1086	1104	1086	1101
02	1102	1122	1101	1120
01	1119	1138	1117	1137
1	1137	1154	1136	1154
2	1142	1164	1142	1162
3	1152	1170	1152	1168
4	1162	1183	1160	1181
5	1186	1207	1184	1205
5½	1203	1225	NA	NA
6	1222	1243	1220	1241
7	1239	1257	1237	1255
8	1249	1271	1247	1269
9	1260	1280	1257	1278
10	1285	1305	1282	1303
11	1294	1315	1293	1312
12	1306	1326	1304	1324
13	1331	1348	1321	1346
14	1365	1384	1388	1366

Each type of cone has a number embossed onto it. In this Orton chart the number of each cone is on the far left-hand column, with each cone's temperature value in the right-hand columns. The chart is divided to represent the two types of cones they have available – 'self-supporting cones' and 'large regular cones'. In addition, each of the two types of cone have their temperature values divided into two further columns – one for 'fast' and the other for 'medium', which indicates the speed of your firing's rise in temperature. The medium firing speed will result in greater heatwork on the cone (and your work) so the temperature at which the cone will bend is lower. If looking for a very accurate top temperature this is important to bear in mind.

Large cones set before a firing in a standard cone stand.

Self-supporting cone.

When the cone is heated and approaching its specified temperature it will bend, curling over completely at its top temperature. If the cone completely slumps and melts, losing its shape altogether, this is a sign that the kiln has gone well above the temperature of that cone. Cones are widely considered by ceramicists to be the best test of a kiln's firing accuracy and can be used to sometimes test if a kiln is under- or over-firing, or even habitually during all firings to monitor the temperature. Cones can also give us an indication of temperature difference between the top and bottom of a kiln chamber, which is a common issue.

If using cones to help us read the kiln's temperature during a manual firing (without the use of a digital controller) we should strategically place three cones in a row near the aperture of a kiln's spyhole so they can be viewed easily from the outside during the firing. This allows us to view the 'curve', or lack of curve, of the cones as they melt. The convention is to use three cones for different temperatures – a 'guide cone', a 'firing cone' and a 'guard cone'. The guide cone will be 20–50°C below the desired top temperature, the firing cone will be the top temperature and the guard cone will be approximately 20°C above the top temperature to tell us if the kiln is over-firing. Of course, having a long soak of more than forty-five minutes may complicate the melting of your guard cone as a long soak can have the equivalent melting effects of a

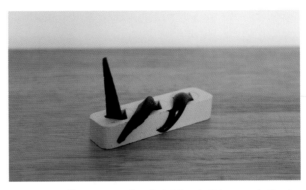

This is a set of large cones after their firing. In this example the right-hand cone is the guide cone, the central cone is the firing cone and the guard cone is on the left-hand side (*see* main text for full explanation of terms). The guide cone has melted completely, with the firing cone melting to just about the right point – it can be observed that the firing cone, or indicator of the top temperature, still maintains some definition in comparison to the guide cone to its right. The guard cone has not melted at all, indicating that the kiln has not over-fired. In this instance I have used the cones to check the accuracy of my equipment rather than help me with running a firing.

higher top temperature, so your guard cone may completely melt and be obsolete as a warning sign to over-firing. This is one instance where testing a combination of cones to achieve your intentions will help you, and a guard cone that is specified to a higher temperature may be better.

Cones should be placed upright in the kiln either using an off-the-shelf setter or can be propped with small amounts of crank clay, which can withstand being fired as wet clay in small amounts. There are many grades of cone, each with a differing melt-temperature, but beware that the temperature for Orton Cone 7, for instance, is different to the one for Orton Cone 07 and so on. *See* Orton Cone Chart.

Using this visual information we can decide to manually turn the kiln up, down or hold the amount of energy going into it in order to make it climb or hold in temperature. If deciding to run a kiln this way it can be useful to have a basic temperature reader attached to a thermocouple in the kiln. This type of read-out will have no way to change the temperature of the kiln but will help us to familiarize ourselves with the rate of temperature increases in relation to the use of the cones.

THE SUNVIC

The sunvic is a kiln's 'cooker' dial. It can be used to control the temperature of the kiln using adjustments up or down to make the kiln climb, soak and cool. Sunvics are usually a simple circular dial with numbers 1, 2, 3 and so on all the way up to 'Full'.

Many kilns now do not necessarily have a purely manual capability for use with just cones. The preference for digital, programmable technology has become the principal way of doing things more recently and if you have a digital controller attached to the kiln this is usually the dominant way of controlling the kiln. Many second-hand kilns have had their sunvics bypassed to accommodate a digital controller but there are still plenty of kilns with sunvics available and these types of kilns can be much less expensive than their fully automated, digital cousins.

Understanding how to control an electric kiln manually can be useful, and a skill that is transferable to other types of firings, specifically ones using other fuels like gas or wood. This is because learning to handle a firing schedule and how to respond to the visual information provided by cones, as well as the colour of the kiln chamber as it heats, may give you insights that will influence your future creative intentions.

When using a sunvic to raise the temperature of a kiln firing, start by deciding how long you would like your firing to be. Below are two example firings:

This is a standard sunvic for a kiln and most follow this format. Their placement on the kiln depends on the design of the make and model of the kiln.

Example 1

A low bisq with a top temperature of 1,000°C – 10–12 hours would be an appropriate amount of time for a firing of this kind. Apply a cautious approach in the first part of the firing – only turning up the sunvic in smaller increments of forty-five to sixty minutes each – with the pace increasing once the kiln is at approximately 600°C; at this temperature the kiln will start to glow red. It is at this point that closing all vents on the kiln is advisable in order to further insulate the kiln and allow for a faster incline in temperature after this point. Below around 450°C the kiln chamber will be black but how the colour of the kiln's atmosphere correlates to its temperature above this will become increasingly familiar to you the more firings you do.

Cones to use for a low bisq
- Guide cone: Orton Cone 07
- Firing cone: Orton Cone 06
- Guard cone: Orton Cone 05

Example 2

A stoneware glaze with a top temperature of 1,260°C – 10–11 hours is appropriate for this type of kiln firing. A similar amount of time can be used as a bisq, even though the temperature is higher, because the rate of a glaze firing can be quicker. Some caution should be taken in the early stages, as with all firings, but a faster firing can be done overall.

Cones to use for a fast 1,260°C stoneware glaze firing
- Guide cone: Orton Cone 7
- Firing cone: Orton Cone 8
- Guard cone: Orton Cone 9

Manually adjustable kilns with just a sunvic tend to be simpler and less expensive than, for instance, kilns with an in-built digital controller, which are now more and more common. However, there is also versatility in controlling a firing manually that is harder to achieve with the use of the more prescriptive formats employed by digital controllers. However, the process of doing things this way can be much more labour intensive, with a large margin for human error, and it is only through trial and error that we can gain knowledge of our kiln and the items we are firing. However, close observation of the kiln can also give you a deep understanding of the nature of your firings.

For instance, ceramicist Akiko Hirai speaks about her first kiln – an inexpensive gas kiln manually turned up and down according to cones but also, crucially, according to the smell of the kiln, which is always a stronger factor in a kiln with fuel that burns, unlike an electric kiln. Nonetheless all kilns and their contents give off a smell and this idea of the kiln's smell being an indication of the arc of its firing is one that is familiar to me. The kiln in the early stage has a very different aroma to the same kiln in the later stages and this can change according to the materials inside it.

As many professional ceramicists' materials settle into a natural rhythm, our senses will give us a more rounded familiarity with our firings – especially as we are deprived of the ability to see exactly what is happening inside the kiln chamber; these additional senses are what we start to rely on. So it follows that a greater level of interaction with your kiln in the early days will give you a depth of understanding. Plus, a cheaper piece of equipment with a manual sunvic and no frills may encourage a less precious, experimental approach – within the limits of safety, of course.

RESPONDING TO PYROMETRIC CONES

Once a guide cone starts to bend, we would lower the power a little in order to steady the kiln's temperature on its climb to the top. By this time the kiln will very likely be on full power so continuing with it on 'full', right up to the top, will result in an over-fired kiln. Once the firing cone starts to bend, the guide cone should already be fully collapsed. Once the firing cone is fully bent it means our kiln chamber is at the desired top temperature and the kiln can be turned off. However, we may want the kiln to soak at the top temperature, in which case we have to find our kiln's sweet spot for holding its temperature, watching that the guard cone does not melt. This will mean looking into the spyhole every few minutes on the approach to the top temperature and then once we are soaking the kiln. This will allow us to check on the curve/melt of the cones. If your last guard cone is starting to bend then this is your cue to reduce the heat going into the kiln even more, by using the sunvic, for the duration of the soak. Once your kiln has soaked for the desired amount of time, switch off the kiln altogether and allow natural cooling of the kiln chamber over the coming hours.

As you can gather, measuring our firings in this way may not give you a completely accurate soak but it can give you an accurate firing temperature with due care and attention. The above description is a general guide but each individual kiln, kiln firing and ceramicist will have different needs so testing must be done for best results.

The above description only uses the example of one set of cones with one sunvic but bear in mind that if a kiln has more than one spyhole it is possible to place a set of cones next to each spyhole for a full impression of kiln temperature throughout the chamber. In addition, many larger kilns have more than one sunvic to control different levels of the kiln and in these instances it can be very useful to furnish each spyhole with a set of cones in order to turn up or down each individual area of the kiln according to temperature fluctuations. This is done because large kilns can have big temperature discrepancies so this facility is very useful.

Cooling the kiln after it has achieved its top temperature can be done naturally with the insulation of the kiln, allowing for a slow, steady cooling (if the kiln has good structural integrity), or it can also be controlled using the sunvic. Natural cooling is by far the more commonly used as there are relatively few circumstances in which very controlled cooling for ceramic materials is required.

DIGITAL KILN CONTROLLERS

Both front- and top-loading electric kilns can be programmed by the same types of digital controllers. There is a wide variety on the market and they can remove much of the human error from a manual kiln firing although they should be checked, at least periodically, for accuracy with pyrometric cones in the kiln chamber. This is a useful diagnostic tool because, as kilns age, parts need to be maintained and replaced and this can help us decipher issues. The placement of cones at both the top and bottom of a kiln will help to establish any cool or hot spots in the firing – *see* Chapter 6 on maintenance for further information about this.

The advantage of a kiln controller is that it gives us a relative fail-safe against missing crucial temperature points in the firing, which is a risk if only using cones and a manual sunvic. I have noticed in recent times that the reliance on digital controllers has increased compared to when I was training, when it was absolutely the norm to always use cones to assess the temperature of a kiln, when to turn it up and when to turn it off, often in combination with a digital controller. This change is testament to the improvement of technology around this area but perhaps also the increased trust that ceramicists have in the technology. In my own practice I have made the complete switch to a fully automated digital controller.

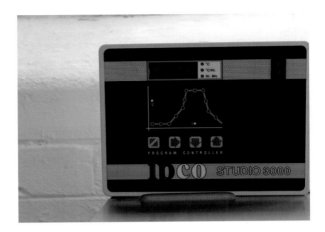

Examples of two digital kiln programmers.

A digital controller will allow you to programme the speed of firing, any soaks or dwell times, and the top temperature of the firing as well as cooling rate, if required. The digital controller will then manage the input of electricity into the kiln's elements at the programmed rate in relation to the temperature of the kiln chamber. In theory this gives a more accurate firing across the arc of the firing cycle rather than just accuracy at the top temperature, which would be the case with the use of cones alone. It is a very good idea to keep an eye on a kiln that is firing but the use of a controller takes much of the jeopardy out of watching and waiting for cones every few minutes as it reaches temperature.

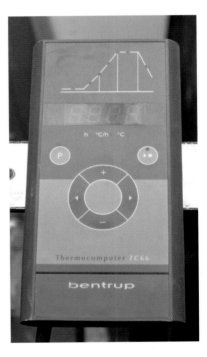

Digital controllers come with more or less facilities depending on your requirements. There are a couple of key 'extras' you will pay more for; one is the number of kiln programmes (for different types of firing) that it is possible to record in the controller and the other is the number of ramps per firing. For most brand-new controllers you will not be forfeiting temperature accuracy for a lower budget, just the number of facilities available. However, any controller is also beholden to the quality of the thermocouple/s inside the kiln so be mindful of, for instance, large kiln chambers with only one thermocouple, or thermocouples that simply need updating. A controller or simpler digital read-out is only as good as the information coming from the kiln chamber, after all. Theoretically more thermocouples inside a kiln chamber will provide better accuracy of temperature – averaging out or allowing the controller to adjust electrical load in different areas of the kiln depending on the sophistication of the system.

A digital controller that has multiple programmes can be preloaded with all the firings you will use without having to key in the firing schedule every time. This is obviously a time-saving facility and may be useful in studios where several people are using one kiln and human error can be mitigated through the use of preset programmes. It is also useful if you are at an early stage and less confident of your firing schedules. I have occasionally seen controllers arrive with standardized firing programmes already keyed in by the manufacturer or supplier on request. However, it is also possible to spend less and buy a controller that has only one programme and so needs to be programmed each time (usually only recording the last firing). You may feel that small adjustments to your firings happen often anyway so having many preset programmes is of little benefit but this is all a very personal choice.

Most controllers will show a digital display of numbers. The number values switch between time and temperature.

Quick Guide to the Segments Found on a Digital Controller

1. Delay time
Delay the start time of your firing. Display: Time

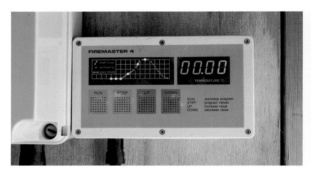

This Firemaster shows a graph that is lit with green LEDs at key points in the cycle of the firing programme. This is a fairly common way to express the firing programme on a programmer although there are variations along this theme. In this image the far-left green LED is flanked by two red LEDs, which indicates that the read-out is referring to the amount of time required for a delay. I have set the kiln with no delay here so, once the programme is set, it will start firing straight away.

2. First ramp
This is the rate at which your firing will rise in temperature to start with. Usually measured in degrees per hour. Display: Temperature – degrees per hour

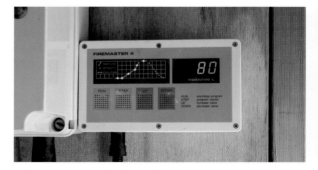

In this image the two red LEDs flank the second green LED on the graph. This means that the read-out is referring to the first ramp so has switched to temperature per hour. In this example the kiln will rise 80°C p/h during its first ramp.

3. End of ramp

Temperature at which the first ramp will end.
Display: Temperature.

This image shows the 'end of ramp' or 'set point' of the firing as 600°C, as indicated by the position of the red LED on the graph. This is where our first ramp ends and we can change the speed of our firing in the second ramp. This programmer has no dwell/soak option at this point, but other programmers often do.

4. First dwell/soak time

Soak and dwell are interchangeable terms and refer to the point at which a kiln firing holds a set temperature for a set period of time. Not all controllers give the option for a dwell in the middle of the firing. Display: Time

5. Second ramp

This is the rate at which your firing will rise in temperature for the next part of the firing. Most ceramic kiln controllers will only have two ramps but it is possible to find controllers with more. Display: Temperature – degrees per hour

In this image the third green LED on the graph is flanked by two red LEDs, meaning the read-out is referring to the second ramp and has switched to temperature per hour. In this example the kiln will rise in temperature by 100°C p/h.

6. Top temperature

This is the maximum temperature that you wish your firing to rise to. Display: Temperature.

In this image a single red LED is at the top of the graph and refers to the top temperature of the kiln, also known as a 'set point' on the programmer. In this example 1,000°C is the top temperature and the end of the second ramp.

7. Final dwell/soak time

This is the amount of time you can ask the controller to hold the temperature at your top temperature. Display: Time

In this image the fourth green LED is flanked by two red LEDs and the read-out has reverted to hours and minutes, referring to the length of the dwell/soak. In this example, the kiln will dwell/soak at 1,000°C for fifteen minutes.

Digital displays will vary between controllers but the principles regarding the way temperature and time are dealt with by a digital controller remain similar across most iterations. For instance, if there are more than two ramps then values will need to be inputted for these in a similar way to the above.

Long Guide to the Segments Found on a Digital Controller

Delay – Most digital kiln programmers will give you the ability to delay the start time of your kiln firing. This can be useful if, for instance, you wish to take advantage of an economical time of day to fire, such as overnight if you have Economy 7, or you wish to load and set the kiln so it reaches temperature when you will be in the studio the following day. Set the delay to 'o' if you wish the kiln to start straight away.

First ramp – A ramp (or segment) refers to the rate at which the atmospheric temperature rises inside the kiln chamber. Most commonly this is expressed as degrees per hour but there are a minority of digital controllers that will ask you for an overall length of firing. However, most ceramic kiln programmers will have at least two ramps so the first ramp is generally slower than the second. A programmer that can accommodate more ramps may be required for achieving crystalline glazes, etc. but if you are buying a kiln for the first time stick with a simpler programmer and upgrade later if required. The first ramp for a bisq firing in a studio setting would be around 80–90°C p/h. However, the slower this first segment can be then the more forgiving it will be to the work inside it so a first segment of 50–60°C p/h could also be used for items that have been handled inexpertly, such as work made during a school's workshop when folded, air-laden and contaminated clay may be present inside the kiln. If the work you are firing is thinly made, using a forgiving, reliable clay and process, then by all means increase the speed of the first segment to around 100–120°C p/h in order to increase efficiency. Ceramic factories have been known to work with greater speeds of kiln firings but bear in mind these environments use industrial materials and methods that have been tried and tested over many years, albeit with an expectation of a certain amount of loss within the firing. In the studio setting we know that some loss is inevitable as each piece is uniquely made, so it is usual to give everything the best chance of surviving the kiln firing with the use of a slower bisq.

First soak/dwell – A soak after the first segment may be used to maintain a set temperature for anything from five minutes to several hours. The advantage of a soak at the midpoint of the firing is often to fully extract all water and gases from the clay body and kiln's atmosphere before allowing the kiln to rise more quickly in the second segment. This can be useful if the clay body is thick, as the water evaporation will be slower as well as there being more potential for gases in a larger volume of clay. It is also possible to use this facility when items have been put into the kiln for a drying cycle before rising steadily to a full firing. Drying cycles are often used to force dry items that are not really dry enough for a kiln firing. This is sometimes necessary because of looming deadlines or poor ventilation in a damp studio during the winter months but not something that should be done habitually as it is bad for the kiln to contain excess water vapour, which will speed up corrosion of the kiln. It is, for the most part, not necessary to soak at the midpoint of the kiln firing but it may be a good idea for large, thick items for the reasons already mentioned; in this case a soak of thirty to sixty minutes is fine at 5–600°C when water extraction is still possible prior to the items turning from clay into ceramic. A soak at the midpoint can also be used to extract all gases from the ceramic as well as the kiln's atmosphere. This can have an effect on glazes, particularly with regard to pinholing. *See* Chapter 5 for more on this.

Second ramp – The second segment usually rises in temperature faster than the first segment but can also be the same rate as the first. For a bisq firing in a studio setting a maximum of around 130°C p/h is appropriate but a glaze firing will be able to with-stand a faster firing of 150°C p/h. It is possible to go faster than this but all temperatures and timings rec-ommended here allow for caution because a faster speed of firing can increase risk to the ceramics.

Top temperature – Your top temperature will be determined by your particular combination of clay and glaze. Bisq temperatures tend to be either around 1,000°C or 1,140°C but glaze temperatures are much more variable. As discussed previously, determine your top temperatures first by determining where your work sits in the stoneware or earthenware ranges and then by narrowing in on your glaze's temperature range.

Second soak/dwell – A soak at the top temperature is more likely to be used than in the middle of the firing. Holding the kiln at the top temperature for a set amount of time can be done for several reasons. One is to either allow a glaze to really mature or melt onto the surface of the ceramic, or to allow a glaze to begin to flow slightly. A soak will also give time for the heatwork of the kiln, allowing the porosity of the clay to become even. What this means is that the clay has an even density from the surface to the core. By definition, the more thickly made something is the more of an issue this can be and a differential in density can result in glaze crazing and other delayed faults because of tension in the ceramic body at a molecular level.

It is important to remember that a long soak often gives the same results as a higher top temperature so you may feel that lowering your top temperature with a long soak to allow heatwork on both ceramic and/or glaze will be sufficient to prevent other problems occurring. For instance, a glaze may flow too much with a long soak at the top of its temperature range so a slightly lower temperature with the same length of soak may help to mitigate glaze flow and run-off onto kiln shelves. For many clays and glazes a short soak of around ten to twenty minutes is all that is required.

At bisq it is more common to use a short soak, or no soak at all, particularly when working with stoneware clays that will bisq low and then go to stoneware temperatures in their second firing, thereby allowing them to mature fully in the second firing. For instance, I will bisq my porcelain to 1,000°C with no soak at all; then the glaze firing will climb to 1,240°C with a twenty- to thirty-minute soak where the ceramic and glaze fully matures/vitrifies.

Cooling – Usually a ceramic kiln firing is simply allowed to cool naturally after the elements have ceased being heated with the electricity to the kiln chamber effectively being discontinued by the kiln controller. It is possible for a cooling cycle to be programmed into kiln controllers with more than one ramp (preferably more than two ramps). Controlled cooling can be attempted using the programmer, particularly one that has more than a two-ramp capability, but there should be a good reason to attempt this, such as glaze response. Natural cooling can take several hours, or even days, depending on the size of the kiln chamber, its insulation and how well packed it is. Near-empty kilns will cool relatively quickly compared to a well-packed kiln load. I have found that a kiln that is evenly insulated and well packed is important because of the cooling, which will be slower if the kiln is full. Steady, slow, natural cooling is always less risky than crash-cooling a kiln.

Hot Orange Azure Baby Cloud Bundle by Tessa Eastman.

Tessa Eastman's studio is set inside Cockpit Arts in Holborn, London. As with many inner-city studios, her space is compact and well organized with a great number of shelves to the ceiling and storage wherever possible. In amongst the tables and shelves she has nestled two top-loading kilns and one small front-loading test kiln – all in a space of approximately 15 × 10ft.

Tessa's work is sculptural and highly coloured. Most often each piece has two or more glazes so her small front-loading test kiln plays a vital role in her practice as her exploration of glaze colour and texture is ongoing. It also serves as a perfect fit for many of her smaller items.

Whilst the electric test kiln plays a role in her development, Tessa does warn against some inaccuracy in it because, although it does give a strong idea of glaze results, it can give differing results to the two kilns in which she fires larger work. This is

Low Density Big Seaweed Cloud by Tessa Eastman.

because the heatwork of the test kiln differs from the large top-loading kilns because their firings are longer with heating and cooling taking more time due to the extra capacity. This has an effect on the glazes because speed of heating and cooling can, for instance, affect the development of the crystalline structure of a glaze, the way it melts and flows, and ultimately the colour can be affected too. Colour can 'burn out' if over-fired, or even if it is heated for a greater length of time than is optimum for the brightest results.

The top-loading kilns in Tessa's studio – one much larger than the other – give Tessa a choice of capacity depending on the size of sculpture but, whilst she always aims to fire economically and efficiently with a full kiln load, there are often just one or two pieces in a single firing. This is because each object has a unique set of parameters with glaze configurations varying from one item to another. This is very different to the priorities of a production potter who is balancing some industrial efficiency with creative intention.

Tessa always begins with a low bisq to 1,000°C and then may end up with both a stoneware and an earthenware glaze on a single piece. This is very unusual because ordinarily a ceramicist works within one temperature range or the other (earthenware or stoneware) – either for single items or, very often, it is a decision that becomes a professional choice that is made early and held onto with some loyalty for a lifetime. For Tessa to be working in this way shows an embracing of ceramic materials for their visual and textural qualities alone in order to make work that is unique and extraordinary.

The way that this is achieved is by first bisq-firing the piece, then painting/dipping/pouring stoneware glaze onto it – covering only the areas meant for this glaze – and firing it to the stoneware temperature required by that glaze. Then, once the piece has finished its stoneware glaze firing, the earthenware glaze will be applied to the areas still left bare and it will be re-fired to the earthenware temperature needed for this second glaze. Tessa essentially works her way from top to bottom of the ceramic firing range in her application of glazes.

Another reason this is unusual is because the application of glaze onto the ceramic body is quite difficult once it has been fired to a high stoneware temperature. This is because its porosity is much lower so it cannot accept the glaze as easily. Tessa's way around this is to heat the sculpture thereby forcing the wet glaze to dry onto the ceramic body more quickly. In our interview she spoke about often re-glazing immediately after a sculpture's first glaze firing in order to harness the kiln's heat thereby evaporating water from the glaze and making it adhere to the surface. This is necessary because, during an ordinary application of glaze, the pores of the ceramic body would absorb the majority of the water within a few seconds. A ceramic body that has been high-fired already has very small pores and this can have the effect of making the glaze 'slide' off its surface.

Once the piece is bisq fired, she is essentially always starting with the highest temperature and working her way down the temperatures required for each one of the glazes she intends to use. This is an adaptation of ceramic methodology, which normally dictates that we only either use stoneware or earthenware glaze on an item. It is very innovative to use this method to facilitate multiple glazes of differing temperatures on a single piece, sometimes overlaying them, re-firing and occasionally over-firing a glaze to achieve a more unique finish. This is a good example of an artist playing with their materials, equipment and educationally-set parameters to create something new. It is very important for this type of practice to exist, to push the boundaries that sometimes keep ceramics in what can occasionally feel like a doctrine of 'shoulds' and 'should nots'.

The make and model of Tessa Eastman's test kiln.

Tessa's sculpture has been fired and is now ready to be removed from the test kiln. Glaze has been applied to the entire surface with the help of three stilts at the base.

The three refractory stilts remain embedded in the piece and need to be removed.

Tessa grinds off the sharp glaze left by the stilts.

CHAPTER 4

KILN READY?

Once the kiln is set up in the studio and ready to go this is the time to begin firing. If your kiln is brand new, or your elements are newly changed, then best practice is to fire the kiln empty to 1,000°C before doing anything else. This will season the new elements making them last longer. Once this is done, firings can begin.

AIR BUBBLES

The presence of air bubbles in clay are infamous in ceramics. These invisible pockets have gained a formidable reputation as the root cause of explosions in kiln firings but I would argue that excess water is the most frequent cause of this firing issue. Whilst air bubbles can be problematic if the clay has been inexpertly folded again and again to create cavity after cavity, or if there is a blatant cave of air that has been closed off, their role in explosions is often overstated. Their reputation, coupled with their invisibility, has become a source of twitching anxiety in many fledgling ceramicists but, in reality, a small air bubble, whilst to be avoided through good wedging or pugging, is not the powerfully explosive force its reputation may lead us to believe.

Having said this, the reason that air bubbles can cause explosions or cracks is because the air inside the cavity expands slightly as the clay/ceramic encasing it shrinks with the heat of the firing. However, a slow firing can prevent some of these issues by giving the air time to seep through pores in the clay before the clay fully shrinks. This is not a total panacea but slower firings can help with this if you feel there may be small issues along these lines. A grogged clay is also helpful for this as the shrinkage of the clay is less than other clays thereby mitigating the problem to some extent.

If you know that you require a part of your design to have a closed cavity then a small, concealed pinhole (or several) is a useful way to allow air to escape during a firing. For instance, you may notice this in some chunkier handles that have been made hollow but, on closer inspection, have a small hole in an innocuous area. The reason for a hollow handle is that it will keep the weight of the piece down – important if it is to be lifted frequently for drinking or eating – as well as reduce the amount of material being used.

Moving Vase by Jo Davies at the Mufei Gallery, Shanghai.

EXCESS WATER

Most clays need to be absolutely bone dry prior to being fired in a kiln. I have seen very thick items take weeks to fully evaporate whereas very thin, possibly slipcast pieces may take just a day. As ceramicists we have to have a way to recognize when items are dry and ready to fire. Most commonly, the way to determine this is through visual assessment and by handling the items. Visually the clay will be the same colour all over, depending on the type of clay, and this will usually be much paler than when wet, but if one area is darker this is an indication that there is some evaporation still required in that dark area. Very often items will evaporate more slowly at the base, or where they are thicker, so turning them upside down, if possible, will encourage faster drying out.

Once the clay is universally pale and looking superficially dry can be a more ambiguous stage to assess dampness and this is where handling the work can become very useful. If our items are stored in an ordinary room-temperature space then we should pick them up and feel them all over, particularly the base or anywhere that air has not been able to flow freely. If it feels cold to the touch then this is often a sign that it is still too wet to go into the kiln. Try to be in the habit of handling your work with clean hands to assess this regularly in order to 'tune in' your fingertips to what this feels like. For me, at several stages in the making process, handling my work is better than sight and this is my main way to 'read' where the clay is in terms of water content for firing, for attaching a handle or for any other part of the process.

Of course, your clay will dry out faster in summer than winter, but if you have a damp studio this will curtail drying at any time of the year; if you have a centrally heated studio (lucky you) then there will be greater consistency throughout the year. However, consider not having your drying pieces in near

contact with radiators as this may cause cracking due to uneven or overly fast drying.

The reason that clay should be dry ahead of its first firing is because the risk of kiln explosions is increased with excess water evaporating at speed from the piece. As mentioned, this is more often the reason for a kiln explosion than air bubbles in the clay, which are most often cited as the cause of this particular firing fault. My personal theory for the proliferation of this explanation is because it shifts blame for an explosion onto the maker, particularly those in a school context (which is where most of us first heard this), rather than the person loading and firing the kiln. The fact is that a water blow-out is much more likely and very easy to mistakenly 'achieve', with even an experienced, professional ceramicist still occasionally opening the kiln to find a pile of rubble, twenty years into their career, because of impatience …

Water blow-outs happen because excess water evaporates fast from the body of the clay. The water molecules expand powerfully into steam with the kiln's heat and if there is too much vapour it will break the clay apart fairly comprehensively. When the water turns into steam there is essentially no longer any space in the clay for it, and so it breaks apart its solid, but brittle, prison. Water blow-outs have a very distinctive look about them – they leave dust and crumbly rubble with no single, obvious fissure. Clays with a high grog content tend to be less susceptible to this than smooth clays with finer particles but caution should be practised in all cases, at least until the sensitivity to excess water can be assessed. This is because tightly packed clay particles make the evaporation of water vapour that much harder.

If you need to fire your work but recognize that your clay may not be fully dry and do not have the time to wait before firing, you can run a drying cycle at the beginning of the firing to extract excess water. However, this should only ever be done once the clay is almost there. Drying cycles are discussed more fully in the following chapter. Completely damp items should simply be left to dry for longer in a ventilated space. When working out how long a project will take it is a good idea to work backwards from the kiln firings at the very beginning of the project's inception, always overestimating the time needed for drying, firing, glazing and possibly re-firing. This way, if things go wrong, very often your client/gallery/curator need never know, especially if you make twice what is needed.

As an approximate guide, a drying cycle would be 30°C p/h to 250°C before going into the usual bisq firing rate after this point. All water is evaporated from clay and the kiln chamber by 600°C, which is one of the reasons why this is the temperature at which all bung and spyholes are completely covered on a rising kiln, but there is no need to extend the drying cycle all the way to, or beyond, this point. Having said this, the variety of possible drying cycles is wide but the abiding principle is that the very early stage of a firing should be elongated to extract water from the clay. Depending on the severity of the excess water content, and thickness of the items, the above example of a drying cycle can be slowed down or sped up.

Very thickly made items (above 1in (2.5cm) thick) are more likely to have an issue with excess water at their core despite long drying times so a slower rate of firing should always be undertaken in the early stages of this type of work. Some of the worst kiln blow-outs I have seen were involving very thick items that did appear to be dry prior to firing.

However, in the majority of cases, excepting very thick pieces, I would not recommend drying cycles on a regular basis and my advice would be to just wait longer. That said, if a long period of evaporation has already taken place then a compromise is the 'preheat', a shorter drying cycle that allows time for the core water to evaporate while the clay is still very porous. A fuller description can be read in Chapter 5.

The reason that drying cycles are not great on a regular basis is because they are hard on your kiln. This is because water in the atmosphere of a kiln wears on it, creating rust in components as well as at the doors and apertures of the kiln if you have a kiln clad in metal. This rust can be the source of iron-oxide dust and will often cause fired-on 'freckles' on ceramic items, which are usually not desirable, as well as the need to replace components more frequently. However, some rust is inevitable during the life of a kiln so maintenance of the kiln in this way is needed.

Firing very freshly glazed items can also create rust in a kiln, especially if items have been dipped in glaze, because the ceramic absorbs the water of the liquid glaze. Best practice is to glaze one day, allow items to dry in the open overnight and then load the kiln on the second day once water has evaporated from the ceramic body. However, in reality, it may be that time and studio space do not allow this so a well-vented kiln in the early stage of a firing will help to force water vapour out of the kiln. Still, the corrosion of components should be taken seriously if excess water is frequently an issue, with visual checks of elements and electrical components being made regularly.

PROTECTING THE KILN FROM GLAZE

Glaze will inevitably be one of the factors that wear out kiln furniture. This is because glaze can be a volatile factor when over-fired, applied too thickly or just in accidental contact with kiln components and furniture. First and foremost we protect kiln shelves by wiping the base of our ceramic pieces to be free of glaze, as well as around 1–5mm up the side from the base, to avoid adhesion to the shelf once the glaze vitrifies at its top temperature. If clearing base surfaces of glaze is not possible, or desired, then kiln stilts can be used to accommodate this. However, be mindful of the maximum firing temperature of the stilts you are using, which are often only graded up to 1,200°C, meaning it is mostly not possible to achieve a full wrap of glaze at stoneware temperatures.

Testing a glaze for its colour, surface and viscosity is always a good idea before piling ahead and applying a glaze bought from ceramics suppliers to precious, finalized work, or making a large quantity of a glaze recipe. Having said that, in the early days, we all do this and so, with some disasters in our wake, we have an understanding of the need for glaze testing. At this stage it is usual to test glazes by applying glaze to tiles that are laid flat on the kiln shelf – there is nothing wrong with this and it will give some indication of the glaze but, with

regard to the maintenance of kiln shelves, it gives no indication of the viscosity or potential flow of a glaze within its temperature range. The most likely scenario, when it is applied to the final ceramic, is that it will flow downward with gravity to a greater or lesser extent and so, of course, we need to understand by how much in order to protect our kiln shelves as well as know what this will look like on our work. Therefore test tiles, laid flat, will not give us this. Many glazes have barely any flow within their firing range but some, particularly if they have colour additions, such as cobalt oxide (the famous blue), will flow more because some colour additions are also fluxing (flowing) agents, especially when applied thickly.

My advice is to test the glaze on an upright tile or, better still, on a miniature version of your piece, using the intended clay, and set onto a waste ceramic or broken kiln shelf in case of glaze run-off while firing. This will protect your good kiln shelves. If you are going to test a lot of glazes then making a setter in the shape of a toast rack from crank clay for test tiles, which can be fired again and again, is a good idea. On each test tile or piece make sure you have differing thicknesses of glaze – one area of one layer, one area of two layers and one area of three layers as a rule of thumb. This will help you to max-imize the information available from the application of the glaze.

Batt wash is another line of defence against glaze. It appears as a white surface painted onto kiln shelves, and sometimes other pieces of refractory kiln furniture, to create a waste layer that will pro-tect the main body of the kiln furniture from glaze run-offs. The theory is that it creates a layer that will chip off easily with use of a chisel and hammer if glaze drips onto the shelf rather than allowing the glaze to be embedded into the shelf itself. The batt wash also functions as an inert, non-melting layer between our work and the adhesive qualities of fired-on glaze that our ceramic items will sit on, and stick to, during a firing.

Porcelain cup by Jaejun Lee.

This layer of batt wash is beginning to be in need of maintenance. The wash has become brittle and is starting to crumble.

However, some ceramicists prefer not to use batt wash at all as they feel it creates work in the form of an additional layer of maintenance of the shelves. This is because it does degrade after a number of firings and so it needs to be at least partially chipped or wire-brushed away every now and then before being re-painted. It will be apparent when to do this when it begins to crack and become loose. These loose chippings can become a liability if not taken care of because they will fall onto glazed surfaces and become fixed into them during firings. It is for this reason that batt wash should only ever be applied to one side of the kiln shelf. An ageing layer of batt wash can be managed if it is contained on one side of the shelf, with any crumbs that come loose during a firing staying in place with the aid of gravity.

More generally, picking one side of a kiln shelf as the top, and one side as the bottom, is a good idea, with or without batt wash, because any glaze drips and detritus will remain contained on one side during a firing. Care should be taken to remove glaze drips as we go but it is not always possible to remove every last bit. Once these types of blemish are removed we can often be left with a 'wound' on the kiln shelf that is crumbly and sheds dust. Again, this is not something we want to fall onto items below

The Olive Tin by Susan Nemeth. Susan has used porcelain in combination with decals onto high-fired porcelain. She fires her work without using batt wash on her kiln shelves.

so having a top and bottom is logical. If your shelves are becoming lightly pockmarked then this may be the moment you decide to batt wash them if you have not already. Doing this will save the shelf and our ceramics because it will lock the dust from these pockmarks underneath it and effectively stabilize the surface of the kiln shelf.

I have personally found batt wash to be a useful addition to the studio, especially when I was running a kiln-firing service in East London. However, if you are taking a no-glaze approach to your work then batt wash is largely without point. For instance, Susan Nemeth, a ceramicist who worked for a long time using coloured inlays in high-fired porcelain, with no glazed surfaces, strongly prefers not to use batt wash. This is partly because there was no glaze so no need to protect the furniture but also because the surface that batt wash creates can degrade to the point of being uneven and could have distorted the very thin, controlled porcelain shapes she was creating at the time. Her preference was therefore to go without batt wash thereby keeping the shelf surface reliably flat.

IS ONCE-FIRING A GOOD IDEA?

Once-firing or single-firing involves glazing raw clay and firing just once without a bisq firing. It is not for the faint hearted. For several of the reasons already mentioned in this chapter regarding kiln blow-outs, it can pose more problems to our kiln because the risk of simultaneously biscuiting and glazing our work can lead to explosions of a kind that can damage our kiln beyond repair. This is because the presence of glaze, if there is a blow-out, becomes all the more messy, potentially gluing itself to kiln elements, kiln furniture and thermocouples alike – all expensive pieces of kit to replace. It is for this reason that I did not allow customers to once-fire when I offered a kiln-firing service at my studio in East London.

Having said that, with more experience of our clay and glaze combination this can be made to work by some ceramicists who swear by it as a simple time- and energy-saving technique. For instance, Annabel Faraday uses this very successfully for her hand-built vessels. By brushing on a clear glaze moments before her firing, and when the clay is completely bone dry, she successfully single-fires her work. It is important to note that when applying glaze to bone-dry clay we should not drench the surface, so any dipping and pouring, if attempted, should be very brief. The reason for this is because the water will disintegrate the body of the clay quickly if left too long so Annabel's technique of brushing on the glaze is advisable. Her use of slabs of well-constructed crank clay is useful in this technique as its versatility, low shrinkage and forgiveness of excess water all play a part in the success of her single-firings. Crank is great for water evaporation because of the openness of its body, which allows for evaporation, and will mitigate water blow-outs.

Overall I would advise great caution if embarking on single-firing, preferably only using well-grogged clays like cranks that will evaporate any excess water easily. Clays with smoother, denser bodies are inherently more risky for blow-outs but, even if the items do not explode, there is the issue that the extra time and materials spent in glazing items is lost. This is because sometimes a bisq firing can also act as a way to weed out items that are not going to make it. After the first bisq firing we can often see cracking and splits, which would indicate that an item is not going to make it through its glaze firing and that no further energy or cost of materials should be spent on it. However, as with all things ceramic, there are options and the choice of separating our firings, or attempting a single one, is a judgement call between the risks and the benefits.

A NOTE ON WATER IN ENAMEL, DECAL AND LUSTRE FIRINGS

Enamel, decal and lustre firings are often the final firings that ceramic items will go through because of their lower firing ranges (enamels/decals: 8–850°C and lustre: 7–740°C). As such, ceramic items needing these firings will sometimes not be done for some time after the glaze firing and, if these materials are being applied to vintage ware then it can be decades since their glaze firing. In the intervening time it is common for ceramic to absorb atmospheric water, which can also happen in a comparatively short amount of time, or even simply through washing. This is problematic during a firing as the water locked inside the ceramic body will evaporate to steam during a firing and often this will happen with such force that it will leave sharp 'pimples' across a glazed surface as it escapes. The best way to mitigate this is to make sure you are returning your item back to the kiln for its enamel/decal/lustre firing within a couple of weeks of its glaze firing. Please also do not be tempted to drench your items in water to wash them ahead of painting or attaching decals. It is best to clean and degrease using white spirit, and no water, for good adhesion of the materials to the glazed surface.

If it has been some time since an item's glaze firing, or you are unsure of how long it has been, preheat your items in the kiln before ramping the kiln programme into a normal enamel/decal/lustre firing schedule. Depending on how much water is in the items, this will help to mitigate potential issues but, like anything in ceramics, there are no complete fail-safes.

If you are buying ready-made glazed items from the factory to decorate then ask the supplier how recently the items have been glaze fired before placing the order, telling them that you intend to enamel/decal/lustre fire them. This is so they can send you items that have been very recently fired as they will be aware of the above issues and will want to make sure you have successful results.

ANNABEL FARADAY

Annabel Faraday moved to her current studio near Hastings in 2017 from her home of many years in Bethnal Green, London. Her work is very much driven by conceptual interests in found objects, the ground itself and place, particularly captured through her use of maps as surface decoration, which she views as being intimately related to the ground. Her time in Hackney was reflected in her work while she was there and then, as herself and her partner spent more time in Hastings, her inspiration has shifted to coastal found objects and inspirations. Images of maps are still a frequent trope in her work, along with images of industrial sites, but they are now slowly shifting out of her practice.

Her studio is a wooden structure detached from the house near the top of her steep garden and overlooking the sea. It is an idyllic spot with space to spread out so she has chosen to house her kiln in a separate building to her workshop. Both were

Bella:Noia by Annabel Faraday.

Annabel's garden studio.

Annabel stands at the door of her kiln shed. The shed is compact but is usefully placed close to, but separate from, her house.

commissioned and built by Annabel. Configuring her work space away from the kiln has mitigated the frequent issues of managing heat (and too fast evaporation of clay) in a small space as well as allowed her to separate herself from the gases created by kiln firings. The 'kiln shed' is set closer to the house than the studio, presumably because this allows for an easier dash to the kiln during a firing to check its temperature. The kiln shed, which is built from breeze blocks, has a small window plus a domestic kitchen/bathroom extractor. When Annabel and I talked about the set-up we discussed the need for an extraction fan in the kiln's shed given that the space is not adjacent to a living or working space and that there is a window for a draw of fresh air.

Annabel creates hand-built vessels and wall pieces using a palette of three clays – Craft Crank, Earthstone Terracotta Crank and Earthstone Black – all of which are reliable clays with few idiosyncratic faults except the Earthstone Black's potential to warp, principally because the extra oxide inside the clay body, which gives it colour, acts as a fluxing agent, making the body start to 'flow' at higher temperatures. Annabel uses technique to work around this such as firing some components of her work, like the 'feet' of some vessels, separately to the higher temperature and then using the lower-temperature firing to fuse them together with glaze.

Her kiln is a top-loading, and well-used, Potterycrafts kiln. In recent times Annabel has begun to single-fire much of her work, that is, glazing greenware and using just one firing to finish the work. This is because, as she puts it, there is no need to do two firings – Annabel fires to stoneware for the glaze and to fully vitrify the body; her surfaces are screen-printed iron oxide and slip, so her main glaze is a simple clear glaze to seal the surface and the image. She brushes on the glaze when the clay is bone dry and immediately before the firing. Brushing on glaze minimizes the absorption of water by the clay.

After a time she realized she was gaining little by bisqing the vessels because both the clay and glaze vitrify in the stoneware range and the clay will accept the small amount of glaze she uses when

Annabel paints glaze onto her hand-built vessels at her studio.

These items are about to be put into the kiln for their once/single-fire.

it is still green. It is important to say that Annabel only decided to single-fire after knowing the strong reliability of her clay and glaze combination so it was absolutely the right decision for her to do this. The benefits are greater speed of process, economy and ecology, but single-firings should not be leaps into the unknown.

In fact, Annabel will still use a bisq prior to a glaze firing if a vessel she is making is required to be watertight because this means she can pour glaze inside the vessel once it has been bisq fired, thereby filling all the pores, joints and corners of the piece for a watertight finish. If this method of glazing was tried with dry, raw, thin clay there is a possibility the piece would disintegrate.

Annabel has honed her process over years, increasing its efficiency and making it even more fit for purpose in terms of her creative intentions. Like all professional ceramicists, she has adapted firing methods to suit her practice in order to make unique and beautiful work.

Annabel Faraday vessels at her studio.

ANNABEL'S FIRING PROGRAMMES

Her single-firing is a hybrid of a bisq and glaze kiln schedule with the top temperature going into the glaze's vitrification range:

100°C p/h to 250°C
175°C p/h to 1,260°C with a 20-minute soak

Her more thickly built items, however, are still bisq fired first and then glaze fired in a second firing. Despite being keen on single-firing she recognizes its risks, even when the clay and glaze combinations are the same.

CHAPTER 5

FIRING FAULTS

Firing faults have many root causes and this term refers more to faults that occur within the duration of a firing rather than always being the fault of the firing itself. Some can be rectified through changes in firing schedules and techniques but many more can only be rectified through material changes in clay or glaze, as well as making-methods. In this chapter we will concentrate on the most common faults and how to improve these through the firings themselves. Please note I have selected faults that can be rectified using the kiln by making adjustments to firings or through generally better preparation for firing.

KILN EXPLOSIONS OR BLOW-OUTS

Blow-outs are caused either by excess water or pockets of air in the clay body. This type of fault will generally only happen during a bisq firing. This is because they are examples of the potential pitfalls of converting raw clay into ceramic and when much of the shrinkage will occur. Shrinkage of clay around pockets of air can cause anything from cracking to an explosion because the air can no longer be accommodated inside the clay that it is locked inside. Similarly, water in the clay body must escape as the clay shrinks but if there is too much water this evacuation of water molecules will be done under extreme pressure, with the fast creation of steam inside the clay having an explosive effect. As mentioned in previous chapters, I have witnessed excess water in the clay body being the greatest risk to items going through a kiln firing.

However, clearly good wedging and pugging of clay will mitigate air bubbles to some extent, as well as good making-practices preventing the importing of air bubbles into clay. That said, simply making sure your items are dry enough before they go into a firing is the first and best thing you can do to ensure their survival in the kiln.

THE DRYING CYCLE

A drying cycle is, as the name suggests, a kiln programme by which we dry out the clay items inside the chamber ahead of the kiln ramping into a bisq or single-firing. We can also use a 'preheat' but this usually refers to a much shorter cycle and is often used as an insurance policy against explosions on ambiguously damp clay. Drying cycles of any variety

Blue and Gold Speak Vase by Jo Davies.

will ensure water is evaporated from the items at the early stage of the firing within the first 2–300°C. Some clays are more sensitive to water blow-outs than others – heavily grogged clays are the least sensitive with sensitivity usually increasing with more dense, fine-particle, smooth clays although there are always exceptions in ceramics, so test for tolerances on this.

TIPS FOR DRYING CLAY WELL BEFORE ITS FIRING

- Drying best occurs in a well-ventilated room with items sitting on absorbent materials like wood. Damp spaces have the effect of elongating drying times, which is useful for extending time to work on the clay but, if looking to dry work for the kiln, move the work to somewhere with airflow. This can be the same in hot and humid spaces as it is in cold and damp spaces although not as bad – trapped, water-saturated air is what should be avoided.
- If drying items at ordinary room temperature then your items should feel similar to room temperature when they are ready to be fired. Get into the habit of touching your work to tune in your sense of where a piece is in its evaporation. The more you do this the more you will be sensitive to the nuances.
- Once the items are loaded into the kiln you can do a drying cycle or preheat before the kiln ramps into its bisq or single-firing. A preheat is often used for items that are thicker or where there is an ambiguity about how damp items are. Very thin items, such as slipware pieces, are unlikely to need this as a slow first ramp will do the same job as the drying cycle or preheat for this type of work (*see below for more detail on this*).
- Open your spyholes on the side of the kiln and bunghole at the top of the kiln for the first part of the firing in order to vent the work of water vapour and gases as the clay decomposes and turns into ceramic. Close all venting holes at around 600°C for an efficient, insulated firing after this temperature point.

Adjustments according to clay thickness, dampness and kiln capabilities can be made to these suggested drying cycles:

- Long drying cycle: 20–60°C p/h to 250°C
- Preheat: 50–70°C p/h to 200°C

Any item that has been made with very thick walls will often do better with a slower bisq firing overall and possibly a drying cycle. We tend to be taught in ceramics that we should not make things more than 1–2cm thick but, very often, this flies in the face of creativity and innovation. The main reason for this 'rule' is to ensure an easy firing and, quite frankly, to limit the amount of material used. These are both understandable and logical, particularly for educational or communal environments. However, if we are in charge of our own firings, and paying for our own materials, then there can be a natural push and pull between these two factors; it is simply a matter of controlling both to suit our ambitions for the work.

Very thick pieces will naturally take longer to evaporate all water so will need longer to do this ahead of the firing, which can sometimes mean weeks of waiting. During the firing they will also

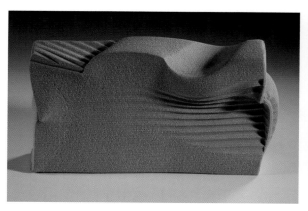

Rome Impressions by Rachel Grimshaw. Rachel works with solid, thick pieces of grogged clay to achieve her beautiful sculptures. This way of working innovates away from the usual method of building ceramic objects thin and hollow.

need longer to evacuate any molecular water in the core of the clay body, as well as gases produced in the decomposition of the material as it is heated. This is because the more material there is, the more evaporation and gases produced by the work, therefore more heatwork is needed and this means a slower firing in order for the heat to really impact on the clay. An item of more than 3cm in thickness should have a preheat to mitigate water blow-outs, a slower bisq firing to ensure heatwork on the clay body to evacuate gases *and* a longer soak at the top temperature to ensure an even structure to the ceramic body.

Alternatively, items that are very thin, like standard functional slipcast items – around 1–2mm in thickness – can take as little as a day or so to dry before firing (dependent on weather and atmospheric conditions in the studio). In these cases a bisq firing can be on the speedier side for a more efficient firing without a preheat or drying cycle. If your work is of this nature then there is little point in extending the firing. In fact, work of this thinness can become over-fired by long firings with a lengthy firing having the effect of overheating the ceramic to the point where the pores become very closed, which can make it very difficult to apply glaze. There are two things at play here: one is that thinner items will heat up more easily and quickly than thicker items so the effect of the same amount of heat on each is different. The second is that a long firing, as with a long soak, can have the same effect on the ceramic as raising the top temperature of the kiln. It may be tempting to over-engineer the kiln programme in order to ensure a safe, fault-free firing but appropriate firings for the work inside them is much more important.

OVER- AND UNDER-FIRING

Over-firing and under-firing are terms referring to a kiln missing its top temperature by the heat either being higher or lower than that expected temperature. Sometimes different parts of the kiln chamber will be under- or over-fired and, if using a larger kiln, this can be more likely an unfortunate feature of that kiln. This usually becomes apparent only once faults start appearing in a glaze. If using the same glaze across all items in one kiln load it can be very apparent that there are hot or cool spots, with the glaze melting differently depending on its position in the kiln chamber; this would be a strong indication that there is an issue in the kiln. However, I hasten to add that this can be seen as a fault in electric kilns whereas gas or other fuel-burning kilns naturally have hot and cool spots, and often ceramicists will work within these parameters. That said, one of the plus points of electric kilns is that the technology has been developed to such an extent that it gives us a more even firing throughout the chamber so our expectations of each type of kiln should be slightly different.

If there are hot and cool spots in an electric kiln then it may be that an element has failed and needs replacing, or that there is an insulation issue in the kiln, or that the thermocouple is faulty. Each of these possibilities should be eliminated before adjusting your firings. Many modern controllers will helpfully give error messages that can help us to pinpoint the fault very quickly so it is worth investing in a digital programmer with this facility. Programmers like this are increasingly a standard and will save you time, money and effort in diagnosing inevitable kiln problems. This is particularly the case if you are paying someone to maintain your kiln for you because the cost of diagnosing problems will soon add up to higher than the extra cost of a kiln controller of this nature.

If there is a small temperature discrepancy of around 10–20°C in different areas of your kiln chamber then your glaze may be able to withstand this although it is not ideal. However, if your glaze is very sensitive and has a small temperature range then you may need to confine items with that glaze to the area of the kiln that will most suit it. This is obviously not ideal if often working with a glaze of this nature but it can act as a temporary solution before other issues are resolved with the kiln.

As mentioned, temperature discrepancies within a kiln chamber are more common in fuel-burning kilns like gas or wood-firing kilns but one of the many conveniences of the electric kiln is its comparatively even temperature; if your electric kiln is showing signs of big differences in temperature accuracy between top and bottom then it is an indication that a component, like an element or thermocouple, needs to be changed, or that insulation needs to be improved.

Under- or over-firing is not such a critical issue for a bisq but can be an issue if it becomes extreme. For instance, on an occasion when an element failed during one of my own low-bisq firings it resulted in the bottom of the kiln becoming much hotter than the top as the remaining, functioning, elements worked harder to bring the kiln as a whole to temperature. The items closest to the working elements became over-fired to the equivalent of 100°C higher than their intended top temperature whilst the items in the other part of the kiln hit temperature. This happened because the thermocouple was positioned closest to the defunct element so did not register the problem and the kiln appeared to have fired without issue.

This was surprising as it may be assumed that a failed element would automatically result in an under-fired kiln overall, but a low bisq of 1,000°C can usually still be achieved when a kiln is down one element. A sign that an element has gone is if the kiln is taking longer than usual to reach temperature so, for reasons of safety and making sure a mis-fire is

not happening, it is worth observing the kiln in the final stages, even if the kiln is fully automated.

In my example above, the result was that the items closest to the remaining working elements over-fired and did not take the glaze at a good thickness when dipped. I noticed this when glazing and hoped that the colour response would be fine but the subsequent glaze firing resulted in a thin glaze coverage, which lacked its usual density of colour after firing. According to my programmer and equipment the bisq kiln had hit its temperature but inside the chamber the heatwork on the ceramic was completely uneven and resulted in poor glaze adhesion in the items that had been over-fired.

When removing bisq from the kiln, try to be in the habit of handling items (with clean hands) in order to gain a knowledge of the feel of the porosity of the surface as this will give you a further impression of how the firing went. If you have used cones in your firings then you will definitively know its temperature but engaging our sense of touch in order to ascertain what has happened is also good practice.

Over-firing during a glaze firing can have some disastrous effects in the form of glaze run-off, colour burn-out, warping or, in extreme cases, the collapse of the ceramic (note that the last example would take an extreme over-fire and is rare). For instance, if using a new kiln, the top temperature that you used in your last kiln may need to be adjusted for the new kiln in order to re-create the same results. It is worth noting that each kiln is likely to give subtly different results in a glaze because finished ceramic objects are always the result of the interaction between all factors involved within the process of making them and this includes the kiln. Testing a new kiln with a few of your items, made using the usual methods, is a good idea, particularly to understand glaze results. The flow, texture and colour of your glaze, if it is very familiar to you, will tell you whether or not you need to increase/decrease the soak, raise or lower the top temperature in comparison to the programme you used in your last kiln, or any other possible change you may be able to make. This can only be done through trial and error.

For instance, if your glaze (whether it is new or very familiar to you) is flowing or even bubbling then this is a sign that either your soak needs to be reduced and/or your top temperature could be reduced. It is much better to test and end up sacrificing a few small pieces to work this out than plough headlong into a full kiln load of items in a new kiln ahead of an important deadline. Cones will also give you an indication of the temperature accuracy of a new kiln but a test of the kind mentioned above will give you much more information about the heatwork of that particular kiln. However, one pitfall with this type of testing, with just a handful of pieces in the kiln, is that a kiln will always cool more quickly if it is sparsely packed so if cooling is a factor in the development of your particular glaze (for example with crystalline glazes) then this should be taken into account.

Under-firing during a glaze firing is potentially not so problematic as it is possible to re-fire the items to a higher top temperature. Some glazes are more happy to be re-fired than others and this can only be known by trying it out. The black manganese glaze I use is very sensitive to this and, if a re-glaze and re-fire is needed, I know I have to do this within a few days of it coming out of its first firing. Leaving it more than this will ruin the glaze completely. Alternatively, the clear glaze I use has no issue with being re-fired, up to a couple of times, weeks or even months after it emerged from its first glaze firing. The reason for the black glaze being so sensitive is something that a scientist, rather than a potter, could probably answer. My assumption is that it may have something to do with the water absorption of the clay body once it comes out of the kiln or that the crystalline structure of the glaze itself continues to evolve on a molecular level after the firing is finished and, once it goes beyond a certain point of development, it cannot be reheated.

So much of what we do as ceramicists is about gathering a working knowledge of our materials and pandering to their various qualities and whims – my practice is no different in this.

Most ceramic items should not be re-fired to glaze/bisq temperatures more than four or five times as it will begin to break down the material. The result can be that the items can become brittle so try to avoid many re-firings as each firing has a further decomposing effect on the material. Plus, the wisdom of this should also be seriously considered from an ecological and economical point of view.

CRAZING

Crazing can be described as looking like lightning-shaped cracking across the surface of a glaze. It can also be circular, in single lines or an isolated crackled area. It can develop within the firing and be very apparent as soon as you open the kiln or it can develop after the firing, sometimes years after the firing, long after it is out of the ceramicist's hands.

However, a 'crackle glaze' that is evenly crackled across the entire surface of a piece can also be a desired effect. The reasons a crackle glaze occurs are the same reasons that cause a crazed surface, as outlined below, but it is important to distinguish between the two. As always, creative intention is key.

If crazing appears in the medium to long term then this can be caused by misuse and mishandling of the ceramic items. It can also be caused by thermal shock if the glazed ceramic is removed from the kiln when it is still too hot, so waiting for a glaze kiln to be lower than 100°C is best practice. If your kiln is cooling too quickly this can also cause crazing and, if this starts to happen to a previously well-firing glaze, suggests an insulation issue in the kiln chamber.

The predominant cause of crazing, however, is

Crazing can be seen here as the crackling of the surface in an isolated area.

from the glaze and ceramic twisting against each other as the glaze continues to try to 'shrink' beyond the level the ceramic will allow. During a firing all materials inside the kiln will expand with the heat and then contract as it cools. By the end of a firing all materials have contracted to a smaller size than at the start, commonly known as 'shrinkage' or 'expansion rate' in ceramics. If the individual expansion rates (the physical size of their expansion and then shrinkage) of the clay and the glaze are very different from each other then the glaze splits itself in the form of hairline cracks – or crazing – to accommodate itself around the ceramic. In extreme cases the tension between the glaze and ceramic can split the item into pieces. Again, this can happen either in the firing or afterwards.

Each material has a unique level it wants to shrink to, with some materials needing to shrink more than others. For instance, porcelain shrinks by around 20–25 per cent whereas other, well-grogged stoneware will only shrink by 3–5 per cent. The amount of shrinkage any given item achieves is partly dictated by the highest kiln temperature the material has gone to – either during its bisq or its glaze – but the shrinkage quoted by a manufacturer for a particular clay will be the one achieved after it has vitrified, that is, the maximum amount it will shrink.

Glazes that are 'low expansion' are ones that expand and contract very little during the firing so are good for reducing or eliminating crazing. A glaze's expansion rate can also be reduced through the addition of various materials to the recipe or simply by buying a low-expansion ready-made glaze, but this only resolves the issue fully if the ceramic that it is applied to is evenly fired with an even core-to-surface pore density. This is because any uneven density in the ceramic can also have a twisting effect on the glaze no matter how low its expansion rate is.

So, for the above reasons, it is more likely that changes to your glaze recipe, or combination of clay and glaze, will do better in resolving crazing. Adjusting your glaze recipe can have a big effect on this issue and there are many ways to do this but, for the purposes of this book, I will concentrate on adjustments that can be made through firings.

It is possible to extend the cooling of your firings in order to mitigate crazing but having to do this suggests that the glaze and clay fit will still be off and that crazing is likely to appear later, once the firing is done. As touched upon, the stability, or lack of it, of your ceramic body may have a lot to do with the type of crazing that appears further down the line. In the past I have resolved one particular crazing issue, when using earthenware clay in combination with various coloured slips and a clear earthenware glaze, by changing from a low bisq to a high bisq and increasing the soak to an hour at the top temperature during the bisq. This had the effect of increasing the density (and therefore stability) of the ceramic body (because of the higher temperature) more than the low bisq but crucially allowed for greater heatwork to take place throughout the clay body by using a longer soak. This was necessary because the work being fired was of a hand-built thickness so it heated more slowly. This had the effect of evening out the porosity of the ceramic body from core to surface and so the ceramic body was stabilized.

In the original tests using a low bisq with no soak, the surface of the ceramic body had had more heatwork than the core, causing its surface and core to twist against each other, which created crazing when the glaze was applied. The increased heatwork in the high bisq, and particularly the longer soak, made for a completely even body that the low-expansion glaze could settle onto and not be twisted and therefore craze its surface. In this example it was the ceramic itself that was still twisting and moving rather than the glaze that caused the crazing so resolving the tensions in the clay body resolved the tensions on the surface.

CRACKING AND DUNTING

Cracks can be caused by issues already raised in this chapter and are most often not caused by the firing itself but by the making process prior to firing, or even the combination of glaze and ceramic if a crack or split appears in the glaze firing. A crack or split of this nature can be seen as a more extreme form of crazing and some of the reasons behind this subject, mentioned previously, will be behind this.

However, it is very common for a pre-existing hairline crack to open up in a firing, or for S-cracks to appear at the base of wheel-thrown pots. The latter will happen if not enough compression has taken place in their making or if the base is too thin or too uneven. Kiln firings cannot often be blamed for these things happening even though they emerge during them. A maker should revisit key moments in their process if many of these types of crack are to be resolved.

However, one way to assess the source of the crack you are dealing with is to consider whether or not it has a sharp edge with a good fit or if it is badly fitting, perhaps with glaze beginning to melt over its sides. A crack with sharp edges indicates that it occurred during the cooling of the kiln, that is, after the item has reached temperature when any crack-ing after this point is more of a sudden split. A crack that has a softer, badly fitting formation indicates an issue in the making process whereas a cooling crack can indicate an issue with kiln cooling being too

fast. This can be directly related to the insulation of the kiln, if the kiln is not well packed or, surprisingly, to the shape of the piece being fired. Cracking due to the shape of a piece can be the result of uneven cooling because an item's width and height are large – which is an indication of dunting.

Dunting often presents as a fundamental splitting of the ceramic through the middle and usually leaves the item in two pieces. It is a cooling crack that will happen at around 570°C on the way down. Most often it happens to items that are wide and/or tall but crucially that have a large amount of surface-to-surface contact with the kiln shelf that it is set onto during the firing. As the kiln cools the atmospheric temperature will drop more quickly than the kiln furniture and ceramic items – as anyone who has opened a kiln of a reasonable temperature according to the digital read-out and ended up burning themselves on a kiln prop can testify. This discrepancy in temperature between air and kiln shelf can result in a catastrophic thermal shock between the top of your piece and its base, which is still in contact with the shelf, resulting in the ceramic splitting itself. This happened during my practice twice when making low, wide (approximately 50cm), circular work when doing my Master's at the Royal College of Art. During that time a conversation with Martin Smith resulted in working out a way to fire future items of this size by setting them on a platform of kiln bricks of the soft, aerated variety, ensuring the bricks were evenly distributed to carry the weight well during the firings. Doing this held the work away from the kiln shelf, allowing airflow underneath the ceramic and making its cooling even. Using this method worked every time because it mitigated any difference in temperature between the top and base of the ceramic item being fired and prevented thermal shock. It is a very simple but effective method that allows items, particularly of width with large surface contact, to survive their firings.

GLAZE RUN-OFF

Quite simply, glaze run-off or excessive, unwanted flow of a glaze is a strong indication that either your kiln is over-firing, your top temperature is set too high, your glaze is too thick or that your soak is too long. If glaze is dripping onto kiln shelves and gluing your items to them then this is a problem. It could also be a simple case of wiping away more glaze from the lower part of your work because the placement of the glaze is the issue. If this is not the case then you could lower your top temperature by 10°C or more, depending how bad it is, if this is within the temperature range of your glaze. You could also reduce your soak time if the glaze is flowing excessively or, conversely, increase your soak time to create more glaze flow on, for instance, a half-dipped cup.

If you feel that there is a risk of glaze run-off then placing your item on a flat waste ceramic or broken piece of kiln shelf can be a good idea for preserving your good kiln shelves. However, I have also seen glaze run-off preserved as part of the visual effect. This can be done by setting a glazed item onto a flat layer of alumina (preferably on a setter or waste ceramic) that will prevent the subsequent drips of glaze sticking to the kiln shelf or surface below but maintain the drip/s as part of the visual effect of the work by allowing it/them to be released at the end of the firing. If using this method the alumina will need to be ground off the surface of the glaze it has been in contact with – *see* Chapter 2 for more about alumina and silica. Batt wash is also an excellent way to prevent glaze run-off from damaging kiln shelves – *see* Chapter 6 for more about this.

This glaze flows beautifully half way down this cup by Jaejun Lee.

SLUMPING AND WARPING

When a piece of ceramic slumps or warps it means that within its kiln firing it has either sagged downwards, lost its shape in some way, gone from circular to oval or it has collapsed in one area to the point where the shape is deformed. The thickness of the ceramic in relation to the temperature of the kiln will have the most bearing on this. So, if this is happening, you need to either lower the temperature of the firing or increase the thickness of the ceramic in the next attempt. Slumping and warping can also be caused by clay that is an uneven thickness so, for instance, a top-heavy item cannot be supported well by an item with thin walls. Therefore the thickness of the item needs to become more structural or the weight needs to be propped in some way during the

In this image of Jeremy Nichols' work in his gas kiln, we can see that he has gone to great lengths to support the handles of his teapots with individually made props. The main purpose of these props is to prevent the handle from slumping downwards in the glaze firing. The prop rests on a glaze-free area of the teapot and has a point at the tip, where it is in contact with the handle, in order to help make it easy to grind off after the firing.

Jeremy Nichols' salt-glazed teapot.

firing. This can be done with a mix of custom-made setters, silica sand, kiln props and ceramic fibre as long as the weight is supported. However, when using supports of this nature it is important to give the clay space to shrink so the percentage and direction of shrinkage should be taken into account when propping an item. *See* 'Setters and Saggars' in Chapter 2 for more detail on this method.

Some clays, such as porcelain, are more prone to warping than other clays, whilst some have almost no movement in a firing at all. Slumping and warping will usually happen around the vitrification point for the clay so if you are seeing this a lot then a first port of call could be to lower the top temperature by 10−20°C if appropriate as well as reducing your soak time if it is long.

If the glaze or clay has a wide vitrification range and your items are slumping or warping when fired to the upper part of that range then lowering the top temperature may help you avoid this problem. For instance, stoneware clay vitrifies between 1,220–1,300°C so if you are using a glaze that has a range of 1,220–1,260°C with stoneware clay and there is slumping when firing to 1,260°C, lowering the top temperature of the glaze firing to 1,220–1,240°C may resolve this issue. This is an easy first fix if it works.

Sometimes a circular item, like a cup, that has warped slightly to oval in the glaze firing can be returned to the kiln for exactly the same firing to resolve this, the effect being that it then 'warps' back to the desired shape in the second firing. Of course, this method may not always go our way but can be worth a try for more subtle issues of this kind.

It is also worth considering working with a possible, almost inevitable, slump in mind when making. What I mean by this is that if we make a shape higher or more proud of the point we want it to be when we are making then the slumping itself will bring it into the desired shape. This works well on more complicated shapes, particularly ones that are top heavy where a downward, vertical slump could be predicted.

Water Pitchers by Jo Davies. When firing these items, I am working *with* the tendency for porcelain to warp. In practice this means that the handles of these pitchers warp the body of the pitcher by pulling it into a more extreme ovoid shape at the top temperature of the kiln firing. Before firing, the items are already ovoid but the firing makes the shape even more so. After years of working with porcelain I have learnt to use what many potters would see as an inconvenient idiosyncrasy of the material to enhance the shape.

Slumping on the base of your item can be prevented by using a setter that follows the shape of the base of the ceramic being fired. For instance, if you are making an item with a curved or undulating base then a setter that follows this form can be a good idea if the piece is settling and slumping during the firing or losing its shape altogether. The effect of the setter will be to support the weight more evenly across the base rather than all the weight bearing down on small areas in contact with the kiln shelf, which are taking all the weight of the whole object. The setter should be of a good thickness for the weight of the piece in order to be robust and can be made from the same clay as the item itself. The setter and your item should be bisq-fired for the first time together so the shrinkage of both are the same. The same setter can then be used for the glaze firing of that piece but is usually then thrown away as it is too small for a new piece of the same kind.

Another method, for a less complicated, concave shape, using clays that have relatively low shrinkage, is to make a setter from crank clay that can be used again and again with either ceramic fibre or silica sand between the item and the setter for extra cushioning and support. This will also allow shrinkage by enabling a sliding effect.

Of course, if you have a flat, unglazed area that the piece could be set onto whilst being fired, albeit upside down or on its side, then this is also a viable option without the use of a setter or props.

GLAZE PINHOLES

Pinholing on the surface of a glaze looks, just as the name suggests, like tiny points where there are pinhead-sized indentations. It is a notoriously tricky issue to remedy as it has a number of possible causes.

Sometimes pinholing can be very subtle, with one or two pinholes across a surface, or a more comprehensive effect. In the second example this may actually be glaze crawling if the 'pinholes' are very large but this is a different issue – see 'Glaze Crawling' later in this chapter. In the case of true pinholing, much is made of this as a fault by many ceramicists. It is true that the potential inlet of water or bacteria into the ceramic body that a pinhole represents is potentially problematic for functional ware. However, I have seen occasions when the pursuit of the eradication of pinholing reaches fever pitch. As previously mentioned in this book, there are times when traditional ideas of 'faults' are not relevant for the object in question and ceramics as a pursuit/hobby/industry can be very wasteful of materials because, for instance, a single pinhole exists on the outer surface of a ceramic object. It is important to remember that the breadth of faults within ceramics became much more prevalent with industrial methods and, while I would not advocate dropping standards, it is important to remember that the value of studio-made ceramics is not in absolute perfection but in an intangible connection of creativity with another human being. I would pre-fer a mindful consideration of what is good/excellent for the object we are trying to achieve versus a slavish, wasteful pursuit of 'perfection'.

Having said this, pinholing can be an annoyance if it is prevalent and, as I say, a potential risk factor in the future usability of functional ware. If looking at using the kiln to clear this fault there are a few things that can be done. The first possibility is that the glaze has been applied too thickly. In this instance, re-firing the glazed pieces and increasing the length of the soak at the top temperature may help to even out the glaze, giving it longer to melt and smooth itself over.

Another possibility is that the gases inside the ceramic body have not fully evacuated during the earlier bisq firing and so their 'escape routes' have left pinholes behind them. If using the same combi-nation of clay and glaze again, having seen pinholing occur in a previous firing, increasing the length of the first bisq firing a little by 10–20°C p/h (i.e. a ramp of 80°C p/h would go to 70/60°C p/h) and/or increasing the soak by twenty to thirty minutes (if there is little to no soak) may resolve pinholes if this is the reason for it in your particular case. Doing this will give more time for the bisq firing to essentially clear out the gases that are creating the pinholes in the second glaze firing.

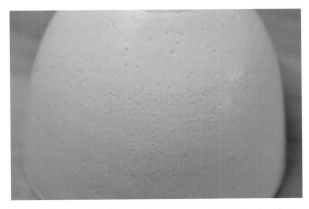
Comprehensive pinholing can be seen across this glazed surface.

The next possibility is that the kiln chamber is not ventilated enough for the gases being released by the clay body during the glaze firing. Like the example of glaze being applied too quickly discussed above, a re-fire will help existing work but, for future firings of the same combination of clay and glaze, a few adjustments to firing methods should be applied. In a studio setting a lack of ventilation can mean that the vents on the kiln are not open for long enough to fully vent the chamber in a way that allows the passing of air across the fired work and therefore the removal of gases. However, during the glaze firing, a combination of full venting in the earlier stages up to 600°C, along with an increased soak time at the midpoint of the firing and the top temperature, can help in the healing of glaze pinholes. Some have also found that a slower overall glaze firing in addition to the use of a soak at the midpoint of the firing will also ensure that all molecular water and gases are vented from the ceramic. The effect of this is to allow gases from the ceramic body and glaze to fully vent from the surface of the ceramics thereby allowing the glaze to vitrify cleanly on its surface.

However, as pinholes can come from a number of causes it is best to try one adjustment at a time because, long term, this will give you the most efficient remedy that will not use huge amounts of energy.

GLAZE CRAWLING

Glaze crawling presents as an area of bare or nearly bare ceramic after a glaze firing, but where glaze had been applied. The glaze has essentially 'crawled' away from its desired position. This is often caused by an area that has been handled and so has come into contact with grease, which then does not allow glaze adhesion. Try to always handle your bisq items with clean hands and glaze them soon after their bisq firing to avoid any dirt accumulating on the porous surfaces. Simply reapplying glaze to the affected areas and then re-firing the item to its glaze temperature can resolve this problem.

Crawling can also be caused by too thick an application of glaze. Re-glazing the areas left bare and then re-firing to the glaze's top temperature can also help to heal over this issue on existing items but, for future work, take care to find the best thickness for your glaze in other items made with the same clay and glaze combination.

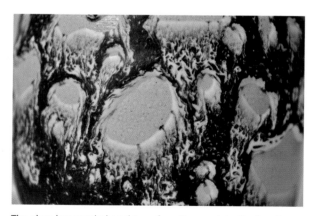

The glaze has crawled on this surface. It was originally glazed all over but, in the firing, bare patches of ceramic have been left clear of glaze.

OPENING THE KILN AFTER A FIRING

One of the final favours we do for our work is opening the kiln at a time that is appropriate for the items inside it. The timing of opening the kiln is an important aspect of your firing because avoiding thermal shock on your ceramic is vital. A bisq kiln can be opened at a higher temperature than a glaze kiln but opening the kiln after a bisq or glaze firing at too high a temperature can be very bad for the work inside it, as well as the kiln itself. Thermal shock has an effect on all materials, some more than others, so opening the lid or door of a glaze kiln that is still reading at over 200°C can result in cracking the glaze and ceramic inside it. Removing the bungs one at a time from around 300°C is possible in order to increase the speed of cooling but the opening of the door or lid too widely and too early will result in much bigger temperature drops that can ruin work with cracks and crazing. If time allows then cooling the kiln naturally without the removal of bungs and early opening of the kiln is best.

Waiting to open a glaze kiln until it is below 100°C is ideal as glazed ceramics will be much more sensitive to thermal shock than bisq items, which can be removed from a kiln at over 200°C. If crash-cooling a kiln remember that the items inside, especially kiln shelves and props, will be hotter than the reading of the kiln's atmosphere from the thermocouple so really good fire gloves should be used – discovering a hole has been burned through the digit of an inadequate glove when holding a hot kiln shelf is a quick lesson in this.

HELEN JOHANNESSEN

This Is How I Feel 2021 by Helen Johannessen.

Helen Johannessen has her studio at Cockpit Arts in Holborn, London. It is a shared space but her area has a decent footprint. Helen uses a plug-in German-built Kittec X Line top-loading kiln that is set at waist height, which is extremely useful to Helen because of issues with her back, and means that she does not have to bend heavily to lower or lift items in or out of the kiln. The Kittec brand is not one of the most well known in the UK but Helen is very happy with the kiln she has from them. I agree with her that the design looks excellent – from the solidity of the lid mechanism, having been hinged with a central pivot point, to the position of the higher kiln chamber and brickwork. Also, many plug-in kilns, despite their descriptions as easily used with domestic sockets, will struggle to reach stoneware temperatures. The reasons for this are several and often down to unique circumstances of a household's electrical wiring plus quality of kiln, but Helen's Kittec kiln achieves stoneware temperatures easily.

Currently Helen works with Parian clay to create sculptural forms made from strips that are delicately stacked in a cylindrical form. Her work has evolved in different directions over the years but her professional practice started under the name Yoyo Ceramics, which became famous for its quirky adaptation of Tupperware shapes.

Having developed Yoyo Ceramics, Helen felt that she needed a new creative direction so at forty-five she applied to do an MA in Ceramics at the Royal College of Art. This is where her work became very sculptural and a new direction was found, with clay itself becoming of much greater interest to her. In her current work the pieces she makes are built tall with a view to certain partial collapse in the kiln. Building within the confines of an inevitable kiln-slump is an interesting way to work as it goes against the way we are taught, that is, to avoid slumping and warping at all costs; fascinatingly, Helen is working with the tendency for Parians and porcelains to slump at high temperatures rather than against this tendency.

This way of working illustrates well the need to continually question the pigeonholing of certain material behaviours, like slumping, as inevitable 'faults'. Helen talks about an excitement around these items being on the edge of collapse, that the sense of peril is actually part of the interest for her and working just within this boundary is an important part of her practice.

One of the practicalities that Helen needs to overcome is the transfer of these fragile pieces to the kiln. Her way of dealing with this is to make the work on the kiln shelves so she simply lifts the shelf into the kiln when it is ready. Doing this, of course, prevents the need to handle the work itself.

Helen, on the majority of occasions, does not glaze this type of work. Instead she either uses the Parian alone or in combination with coloured slip and has chosen to simply high-fire to 1,240°C where the clay will vitrify. She mentions that she likes the 'glassy' finish of Parian on its own and states that this is one reason for its use, instead of porcelain, which has a slightly different finish. She also mentions that Parian fluxes at a lower temperature to its porcelain cousin, giving her more scope for slumping in that firing range but also for fusing the clay together at the lower end of the stoneware firing range.

This way of working is an example of the choice to not glaze as well as the use of slumping as inherent parts of the creation of the work. Not all ceramic needs to be glazed, even though a majority of it will be, but there are many clays that have beautiful surfaces when fired to the right temperatures so, in this instance, Helen has chosen to use the satin surface of Parian as the main surface of her work. However, it is important to note that the results would not be the same if she fired to a temperature lower than the vitrification range of Parian because this is where it starts to flux, thereby fusing the strips together.

Even though Helen mainly does not use glaze, she still fires her work to bisq and then high-fires to 1,240°C in a second firing. This is in order to keep her options open after an initial low bisq because at that point she can not only refine the surface by sanding it but will also choose whether or not to break off parts of the piece and even reconfigure them within the work. The reason this works is because, when fired to 1,000°C low bisq, the ceramic is still quite brittle but not so brittle that it is too fragile to handle. With this in mind she may also stack two or more of the cylinders together to create taller pieces than is physically possible with raw clay. Once they go through their second 1,240°C firing these reconfigured stacks and pieces will fuse together. Parian is sometimes known as self-glazing because of this particular material quality so it is important to remember a clay fusing together in this way is a rarity and partially the responsibility of the base materials making up Parian; it is therefore highly unlikely in most other clays.

HELEN JOHANNESSEN
FIRING SCHEDULES

Low bisq:
80°C p/h to 400°C
150°C p/h to 1,000°C

High fire:
120°C p/h to 360°C
160°C p/h to 1,240°C
With a 10–20-minute soak if glazed

Helen's Parian sculptures are built at her desk on kiln shelves in order to avoid handling them when loading them into the kiln.

The sculpture is about to be lowered into the kiln using the kiln shelf as a tray.

The sculpture is now in place. Note that this kiln is raised up to a height that is easier on the back, and the armature of the lid design helps in the smooth closure of the kiln. This Kittec kiln is certainly one of the most ergonomically designed kilns I have seen.

CHAPTER 6

KILN MAINTENANCE

Through general use all kilns will start to become ever more tatty. There is great pressure on the materials making up the kiln simply because of extreme heat and cooling alone. By adding various ceramic materials into the mix, some of which are volatile, there becomes a need to maintain the kiln regularly. This ranges between some quite simple, regular maintenance to more complex replacement of kiln components. Exactly where your confidence in doing your own maintenance sits on this spectrum is very individual but there is a large amount that can be done by a ceramicist to both mitigate problems as well as fix faults.

KILN CLEANLINESS

The inside of the kiln chamber will accumulate ceramic dust, glaze detritus and kiln brick powder; plus, if using silica or alumina, this will be another form of contaminant. Best practice advocates vacuuming the kiln just before loading it. At this point the kiln will be cool, the dust will have settled and we can load the kiln full of new items in the knowledge that the kiln is as clean as possible. However, the reality is that most ceramicists vacuum their kilns a little more infrequently, depending on the nature of its use. That said, if there has been a blow-out in the kiln then vacuuming it after this is absolutely necessary and the same can be said when using silica sand a lot.

The point of vacuuming the kiln is to prevent materials that contaminate, for example materials that will fuse onto glaze, from moving around inside the kiln chamber while firing as well as preventing materials, particularly those with a lower melting point, from settling onto kiln elements and speeding up their demise. For instance, a glaze shard landing and then melting onto an element during subsequent firings can cause the element to break. Your elements will need to stay clean so that their coating of oxidation remains intact and uncontaminated, which will help them to remain efficient and increase their life.

The way to vacuum a kiln is to take the nozzle and, starting at the top of your kiln, run the nozzle along each niche housing each element; if you have 'crevice tool' or 'brush tool' fittings for the vacuum then even better. It can help to give the element a light jostle with your fingertips (only when we are working with a cool kiln) to loosen any detritus that has caught in the brickwork and elements, allowing for easier vacuuming. Work your way down from top to bottom, getting in all the corners of the kiln but taking great care not to vacuum away any of the ceramic fibre lining the lid/door of the kiln

Pouring Bowls by Jo Davies.

or on the base, if there is any. I have found that it can be useful to use the upholstery/brush fittings of the vacuum to go over the flat brickwork of the lid/door, walls and base. Occasionally you may be feeling very thorough and the top of the outside of the kiln will be cleaned too – this can be useful as an occasional job, particularly when a moving part like a lid or damper can, depending on its design, end up depositing all sorts of unwanted contaminants inside the kiln. Rust in particular is an issue here but please *see* 'The Rusty Kiln' section in this chapter for more about this.

BATT WASH

Batt wash (also known as kiln wash) is a line of defence against glaze that appears as a white surface painted onto kiln shelves as well as other pieces of refractory kiln furniture. It is painted onto the surface of kiln furniture in order to create a waste layer that will protect from glaze run-offs embedding themselves into kiln shelves and other kiln furniture. Batt wash does not have to be used but it can be valuable as part of our arsenal in protecting the kiln. However, if choosing to use batt wash, it does require some maintenance.

Batt wash can be bought as ready-made from most ceramic suppliers and is of a good quality. It can be bought in powder form and mixed with water to a consistency that is preferable to the individual, usually to a thin consistency. Sieving the batt wash in a similar way to glaze (albeit using a more coarse mesh) may be helpful in straining any lumps but mixing, soaking overnight and then further mixing will give a similar result. Once it is mixed to a milk/water consistency – having it too thick will make it harder to apply on larger surface areas – you can simply brush it onto your kiln furniture liberally, although try to keep it as even and flat a layer as possible. Allow to dry well before placing items to

be fired onto the surface but the newly batt-washed items do not need to be sintered alone in the kiln before being used for a loaded firing.

A layer of batt wash will last for quite some time before needing to be maintained or topped up. How frequently depends on the way we are using our kiln, as well as the temperatures involved, but visual checks of the surface for chipping and cracking of the batt wash layer are the main way to assess this. The principal issue with batt wash is that it will become brittle and break away from its surface eventually so it is for this reason that we only ever batt-wash one side of a kiln shelf. This ensures that loose pieces of older batt wash do not rain down on our glazed work from the underside of a kiln shelf.

Once a layer of batt wash is cracking up or has glaze run-off on its surface this is the time to chip off the loose batt wash and reapply. You will need a small but heavy-duty chisel, hammer and grinding stone but please also make sure to use safety goggles for this job.

When cleaning up glaze from kiln shelves it is very important to wear protective goggles as the shards will fly in any direction. Place the chisel where the glaze meets the kiln shelf at a 45-degree angle or less; chip gently but firmly by hitting the chisel with the hammer. I have found that doing this on the floor rather than the studio table tops is the best place for this job. The reason for this is that the floor is a solid base to set your shelves (a towel or other soft material underneath them can protect the shelves as well as lessen the noise for neighbours) but it will also mean that any shards or tiny chips do not end up on surfaces that will then have clay wedged or worked on them. After these types of jobs we do our best to thoroughly clean but the tiny, razor-edged shard that embeds itself in the table top can appear again weeks later. Having said all that, this is one of my favourite maintenance jobs in the studio, and is particularly satisfying when the glaze remnant comes away cleanly in one.

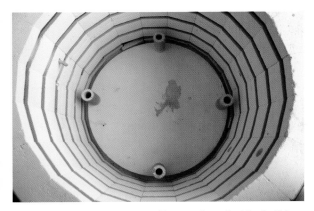

Here we can clearly see an area of batt wash on the kiln shelf that needs to be cleaned up and reapplied. Note that the shelf is only batt washed on the top side and is always used this way up.

Hammer, heavy-duty chisel and grinding stone for removing glaze remnants from kiln shelves.

Once the glaze is gone from the kiln shelf, or the worst of it has been flattened over, and any sharp edges have been chipped or ground down using a grinding stone, then it can be a good idea to lightly wire-brush away any loose pieces of glaze or old batt wash before re-painting fresh batt wash back onto the kiln shelf. If wire-brushing batt wash, take care to wear a dust mask. Any trace remnants of glaze on the shelf can then be painted over by the batt wash and will become an inert surface again so take care to make sure these blemished areas have good coverage. Once this is done the kiln shelves can continue to be used as normal.

THE RUSTY KILN

Most electric kilns are encased in a metal chassis to increase their durability. Although kiln bricks are doing the majority of the work in terms of insulation during the firing, they are very soft and the metal allows for the placement of parts such as levers for dampers or sunvic controllers. However, the expelling of water vapour from key points on a kiln during a firing can also create rust in localized areas on a kiln's metal chassis. Venting holes, and around the kiln's lids/doors, are areas particularly

This top-loading kiln is suffering from some rust damage caused by excess water vapour leaving the kiln chamber around the lid. Making sure your work is bone dry before firing and leaving venting holes open until 600°C will ensure that this type of damage is slowed down.

susceptible to this and will, at some point, begin to accumulate rust as the kiln is used more. More concerningly, rust can accumulate in the area of the kiln that houses electrical contacts and hardware – or control box – so this is another reason to periodically open this part of the kiln and gently vacuum these areas in order to remove rust and dust as well as allow for a visual check of the components.

The first and foremost way to prevent rust is by firing work that is completely bone dry before it is loaded into the kiln, as mentioned in previous

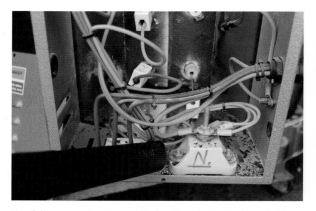

Carefully vacuuming the rust that gathers in the kiln's control box. Notice the rust starting to accumulate on the contact points and components in this area.

After vacuuming.

chapters. However, there will always be some water locked inside the clay body, or water that has been absorbed into ceramic pores after glazing, which will need to be allowed to evacuate the kiln; venting the kiln chamber well by keeping the bunghole/ spyholes open until 600°C, when all water has evaporated from the clay/ceramic/kiln chamber, will reduce the accumulation of rust around areas like lid/door seams by allowing the vapour to escape cleanly.

If rust is allowed to become extreme then one possibility is that the structural integrity of the kiln is compromised or, at the other end of this extreme, small amounts of rust (iron oxide) flakes drop onto glaze and fuse thereby peppering it with brownish specks. Neither situation is desirable so the gentle vacuuming of loose flakes should be done from time to time. Rust is very difficult to prevent completely so, theoretically, a layer of rust can help prevent even more rust developing. This is because exposing fresh metal, by completely eradicating existing rust, can hasten the metal thinning even further because we are essentially offering up more metal to turn to rust. Overzealous wire-brushing of rust can, in the long term, make the situation worse. Making sure that rust is stable and not shedding is the main

priority; a kiln can work perfectly well with just this as a maintenance solution for this particular problem. However, it is also possible to paint rusting areas, in order to further seal them, with a high temperature metal paint that can withstand 600°C or more. These types of paints are usually advertised as being appropriate for woodburning stoves and all manufacturer's instructions should be followed to ensure good adhesion. Please note that ordinary metal paints will not be able to withstand the heat and should not be used on kilns as they will flake away easily.

Rust will be an inevitable part of your kiln over time if it has any metalwork attached to it. The prevention of rust is a Sisyphean task so whatever path you choose to keep on top of it there will be more to come later. However, kilns that are simply allowed to rot away to rust are a sad sight, not good for your work and potentially make the kiln ineffi- cient. So it is worth paying periodic attention to this in order to keep your kiln in working order because its presence in your electrical contacts can create kiln misfiring and contamination inside the chamber that affect your work.

KILN ELEMENTS

The elements in the kiln are made from Kanthal and Kanthal A1 wire for higher-temperature kilns but some kilns that are only graded for lower temperatures may have nichrome wire elements. Either way they are the principal source of heat for an electric kiln firing so they are built to withstand a huge amount of pressure and all need maintenance. Elements are also, by far, the component in the kiln that needs changing most frequently. Many ceramicists will want their kiln doctor to deal with all aspects of the kiln but many others will have a knowledge of the issues around the elements that means they can diagnose problems and bring in appropriate maintenance to mitigate issues. If you do decide that always using a professional kiln doctor for all maintenance is for you then it will still pay to have a basic knowledge that results in an informed conversation prior to a costly diagnostic visit.

Firing to stoneware temperatures regularly will always be harder on the elements, giving them a shorter life, than only firing to earthenware temperatures but there are a few regular maintenance jobs we can do to help the elements last as long as possible.

Simple vacuuming of the elements and their housing inside the kiln (without removing the elements) is the first port of call in preventing glaze or other materials from fusing onto them. Glaze material that fuses onto the elements can impede electricity from running through them efficiently or snap the wire altogether, so keeping on top of this is important. Blow-outs or other firing faults, as well as dust from kiln bricks, can leave particles of material moving around the kiln and landing on elements so this simple maintenance can really increase the elements' life if done regularly.

If you have a brand-new kiln, or just new elements, the first firing is needed to sinter them and so this firing should be run empty. This first firing should be to Orton Cone 06 or just above 1,000°C and completely empty of ceramic materials.

New elements are shiny, smooth and malleable before their first firing but, after heating, they develop a layer of oxidation, which appears matt and pale grey, as well as becoming much more brittle when cold. The pale grey colour that develops in that first firing is a protective layer and should be allowed to develop in the first firing without disruption by the gases or particles produced during a ceramic firing. Firing new elements with ceramics will interfere with this oxidation and may hasten the ageing of the elements. Some manufacturers also recommend that the brickwork of new kilns is vacuumed before their first firing because of vibrations from the journey having deposited brick dust onto the elements, which also interferes with the oxidation layer in the first firing. The same could be said for any recently transported kilns. The more that elements are fired the more this oxidation layer increases, penetrating the core of the element, and eventually it will be the reason for a lack of electrical efficiency as the electrical resistance in the element will build up with each use.

One of the most common issues with elements is the possibility of them sagging from their housing niches. This happens because the wire softens and expands as it heats up so it may 'escape' its housing. After just one or two firings, elements will start to become much more brittle so simply pushing them back into their housing often results in a snapped element that is then useless and will need to be replaced. To prevent elements from sagging we can pin them into their niches with loops of Kanthal wire at regular intervals along their length when being installed. Alternatively, when an element is completely brand new, prior to installation and its first firing, an element can be stretched so it is slightly long for its housing. This will brace the element into the back of the niche and compensate for some of the natural movement and softening of the

This element is sagging where the brickwork in the kiln has broken away. This is because, at high temperatures, Kanthal wire softens so it is important to keep the brickwork around elements in good condition.

element as it heats. This latter method works best for barrel-shaped kilns but, of course, doing both may be best for the shape of your kiln.

If your elements do start to sag then it is possible to tease them back into place but only by heating them with a blowtorch and manoeuvring them gently back into place with two pairs of needle-nosed pliers. Heat is needed in order to do this because cold elements are very likely to snap when an attempt is made to bend them. The heat softens the element just enough to make it malleable in the area that needs to be adjusted and mitigates the possibility of the element snapping. Take care to heat the area of the element that needs adjusting, as well as the area a few inches to either side of the sag. This is in order to keep malleability in an area that is wider than is absolutely necessary to avoid the element snapping. Then, with a pair of pliers in each hand, pincer the wire in two places on the sagging area of the wire and gently push it back into its housing. Do not attempt to move the element with your hands as it will now be extremely hot.

A small hand-held blowtorch obtainable from many DIY shops is fine for this job but all manufacturers' instructions for these items should be

followed for safety and best use. Bear in mind that this should be slow work and you may need to reheat the wire between each burst of manoeuvring depending on the size of the sag. Heatproof gloves and goggles should also be used, as well as hair being tied back, and no scarves or draping clothing worn – this is of importance with all kilns when doing this job but particularly if working on an element in a top-loading kiln.

Once back in place you may then want to pin this part of the element using one or two Kanthal wire loops. Any pinning should be securely against the back wall of the element's housing so using the end of your needle-nose pliers to access this may be one of the better methods you can use to push the loop securely into the kiln brick behind. The brick is very soft so a relatively small amount of force can be used to do this and aiming for the seam between bricks is better.

It should be said that this method of heating elements to return them to their housing niches may be a little controversial but, from a ceramicist's point of view, being able to keep a kiln running on a low budget is one of several priorities. If your elements are sagging frequently then it may be time to change them over or to consult a professional on the reasons why they are doing this – age of element, design of the kiln or method of installation can all play their part.

However, sagging elements do not mean a kiln cannot function. Many kilns will function for quite some time with this issue present but the elements will eventually snap if not taken care of. Sagging elements can also be awkward when loading the kiln because they take up space in the chamber and can touch items being fired, which is not desirable. A certain amount of time and effort will be spent in avoiding them when packing the kiln and if the element ends up sagging so far that it touches another element there is a good chance that this will cause one or both elements to snap. The same is true if it comes into contact with a glazed item, where the

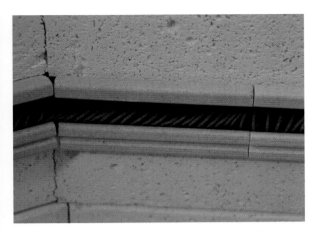

The element here is starting to bunch together although it is not too bad at the moment. If allowed to become very bunched together this can create hot spots in the kiln.

melting surface will disrupt the element and cause it to snap or leave a glaze blemish on the element that impedes electricity from running through it. Either way, the element is gone and will need to be replaced.

When elements bunch together, with all their loops becoming tightly packed, this can create a hot spot along the element and, in turn, in that localized area of the kiln. If it is very bad then it may be better to replace the element or, if not so bad, the individual loops of the element can be teased apart a little using the above method of heating and pushing gently apart using needle-nose pliers or a flathead screwdriver.

Elements can also just age to the point where they are running very inefficiently and take a long time to make the kiln reach temperature. Old elements tend to have a very pitted surface, which is a sign that their oxidation layer is becoming very thick compared to their electrically conductive core and so the electrical resistance is increasing. The elements may also be visibly losing their shape, along with being slow to reach temperature, so if you have all of these symptoms it is time for a new set of elements.

Hopefully a full set of elements will age at a similar rate but it is possible to change just one element at a time if just one fails. However, changing the full set is better for an even firing. Changing just one at a time can also mean going through elements slightly more quickly because of the difference in efficiency between the old and new elements. This will force one or more elements to work harder, thereby ageing them faster, but a full change is more costly, even if changing them yourself. In my own practice I used to just replace single elements but, in later times, I have seen the benefit of a full change of the set so my feeling is that this decision is down to short-term versus long-term budgeting and whichever is your priority at the time. On this front all advice should be thoroughly researched before being acted on, especially from those who have an interest in a greater amount of work needing to be done when a quick fix that will keep you going for a while longer would be fine.

CHANGING THE ELEMENTS

Doing your own element change on a kiln is not rocket science but caution should be applied at all stages. The below advice is general and can be used as part of your research into your particular kiln's requirements in conjunction with specific technical advice from the kiln's manufacturer. If you do not have the kiln's manual then please search for this online initially, as they are often made publicly available, or contact the company who produced the kiln directly to acquire a copy. In this chapter I have used my own kiln as a specific example in order to illustrate important points around changing elements, but it should be noted that each kiln design will have differing requirements.

The tools you will need are screwdrivers of differing sizes, needle-nose pliers, regular pliers, wire cutters, possibly a hammer, almost certainly some WD-40 (or equivalent) and your vacuum cleaner so

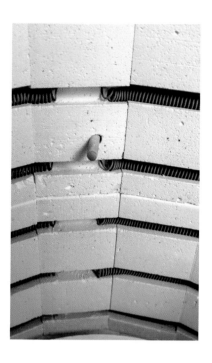

In this image of the elements in a top-loading kiln, one element counts as two rows of wire as it will navigate the circumference of the kiln twice.

Here we can see inside the control box. The top element enters the kiln through the hole on the left and is connected to the red 'live' wire using the white block 'connector'. The element follows the circumference of the kiln and re-enters the control box through the upper right-hand hole. On the right we can see that another connector has been used to 'connect' it to the second half of the element, which then re-enters the kiln chamber through the bottom right-hand hole. This then follows the circumference of the kiln and returns to the control box and connects to the 'neutral' wire. This is a single element despite being cut in two halves. One way we can observe the start and finish of an element is by seeing that the live (always red or brown) and neutral (always blue or black, although here it has faded to grey because of the heat from firings) wires are attached to each end of the element.

you can clean the inside of the panel/control box before closing it up.

Before starting this job make sure that you have the correct set of new elements for your kiln's make and model and that those elements have been produced by a trusted manufacturer – often going to the company that made the kiln is a good place to buy new elements but many kiln doctors produce their own. In one kiln different elements are rated for different amounts of electricity (ergo heat) so it is important to position the correct gauge of element in the right position in the kiln. New elements should therefore arrive labelled.

For instance, in a top-loading kiln with four elements, the middle elements are differently rated to the ones at the top and bottom so it is important to put the right element in the right place – it is for this reason that all elements should arrive labelled so do not discard these labels until the very last minute in order to avoid confusion. In a top-loading kiln, the labels will say 'bottom', 'lower middle', 'upper middle' and 'top', which is hopefully self-explanatory.

In a front-loading kiln the elements are numbered. This numbering always starts from 'number 1' on the top left-hand side of the square/rectangular kiln chamber and works its way down and around the kiln in an anticlockwise direction all the way until the last element, which will be next to the 'number 1' element.

Remember that a single element may loop around the kiln twice in a top loader, or have two rows in a front-loading kiln, but count as one element. Most commonly, in order to find where a single element starts and finishes, trace the wire element from its entry into the kiln chamber all the way to the point where this element exits the kiln chamber. This may just follow one circumference of the kiln but often the element will follow the circumference twice. However, there are exceptions to this, for instance when one element (or one electrical circuit) is in two parts but connected using an electrical connector within the control box – *see* above image.

Control box for top-loading kiln.

Control box with front panel removed. We can see that:
- This kiln has three elements.
- The thermocouple is below the top element with orange wires leading to it.
- Brown and red wires are live; blue wires are neutral.
- Yellow and green wires are the earth wires.
- Electricity comes into the kiln from the right-hand side, along with connections to the digital kiln programmer.

In this kiln design by Potclays, the electrical circuit has a switch at the top left of the control box – two black buttons sitting on top – which is switched to 'on' when the lid is closed; this pair of black buttons close to 'off' when the lid is open because the hinge mechanism will close them. Many kilns have a manual way to do this with a key that is twisted at the front of the kiln. Again, there are many designs for this type of switch so make sure you understand how yours works.

If you are buying just one or two elements then it is important to specify to your supplier which one/s you need so you have the correct gauge for the position. The kiln's manufacturer may also be able to guide you on this but, failing this, speak with your kiln doctor. This is an instance where bringing some knowledge to the table when seeking confirmation from an expert is very useful in finding the information and parts needed. My experience is that most are very patient and quite used to working with a creative community with a different skill set to their own.

Firstly, when embarking on changing elements and ready to replace the old ones, do not do anything else until the kiln's isolator switch is off, along with all other circuit-breaking switches on the kiln. Once this is done we can undo the screws of the control box or panel, which houses the elements' connectors, and open it up.

Exactly where the control box/panel is will be evidenced by where the elements are exiting the kiln chamber. Once this box/panel is open it is usually my habit to take a few detail photographs as a reference point for later – a good idea, especially if this is your first time embarking on this job, in order to reproduce the wiring and layout as it was originally done by the manufacturer. It is important to take note of the existing design of the layout and wiring of your kiln through photography, as well as any schematic drawings you have from the manufacturer, and simply change like for like.

When you are ready, undo the element connectors and then remove the old elements from the kiln chamber carefully and without damaging any of your kiln bricks. You can take out all elements in one go or do this one by one, that is, remove an element and replace it before moving on to the next one to do the same thing, if replacing the whole set. My own preference is for the latter method. This is so that when I am changing the full set, the job itself does not become an overwhelming visual mess of wires and it is easy to see where connections should be replaced as there are fewer that need to be reconnected at any given point. Life has a habit of continuing to happen when I sit down to do this job – the phone rings, a delivery is at the door – so it is important to have a method that can be broken into smaller steps because breaks in concentration happen.

When removing your elements it can be easy to damage the kiln's brickwork, especially if the old elements have been pinned into position, so it is a good idea to methodically remove the pins with needle-nose pliers or by carefully using the element itself to pull each one out. However, please only use this latter method if discarding the element being removed.

Before you begin to position the new elements, a certain amount of clean-up of the kiln chamber and control box is required. Vacuuming each element's housing niche when it is empty, and when you can access it fully, is best practice. Returning to the panel/control box, a visual inspection of the ends of the wires and the cleanliness of the inside of this area is necessary. It is normal to see a certain amount of superficial wear and tear from the heat of the kiln but the vacuuming of rust and dust is good to do at this point as well. The ends of the wires in contact with the elements can suffer with oxidation, making them quite brittle and worn, so occasionally snipping the ends off and stripping around 2cm of the sheathing to reveal new metal will make for a much better electrical contact – if either using the wire in direct contact with the element or if using an insulated ring terminal.

Make sure all your element connectors are in good order, not burned out, cracked or any other issue. Some manufacturers will recommend the connectors are replaced with each element change but, in my experience and in consultation with kiln doctors, this is not necessary. However, a periodic changeover of this component is worth doing. The design of your connectors differs depending on the make of your kiln but they are always made from brass (sometimes with ceramic casing). These items are very robust but do sometimes need some WD-40 to unscrew more easily. A quick wire-brushing may be all that is required to rid them of residual rust and carbonization, if any. These items do not need to be spotless but decent cleanliness in these areas will help with efficiency and keeping the electrical contact sound. One possible issue with connectors that have ceramic casing is that the brass can become teardrop-shaped in profile rather than circular – if you see this then it is a sign that they need replacing. Please do check that any replacements are graded for the voltage and heat they will need to withstand. Your kiln's manufacturer is often a good source of these parts and information. For instance, Potclays in Stoke-on-Trent is very good in offering spare parts for much of the equipment they sell and they happily offer advice to customers looking to problem-solve so please do use resources like this.

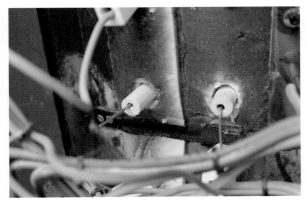

On the left one end of the element can be seen through the lead-in tube with the connector removed.

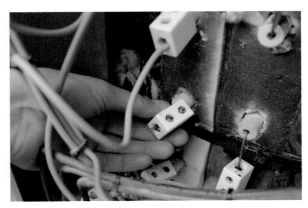

To connect that end of the element to the electrical circuit open up the screws on the connector and slide onto the end of the element, bracing it against the lead-in tube.

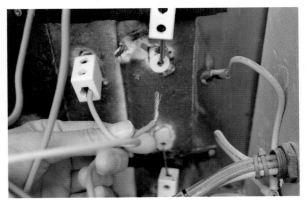

Before replacing the wire, check that it's in good condition without rust or other contamination before also sliding it into the same connector at the end of your element. Each element should have a live (red/brown) wire at one end and a neutral blue/black wire at the other end of the same element.

Do up the screws of your connector tightly, making sure that it remains braced against the lead-in tube. Repeat this process with each element, making sure that a red/brown live wire is connected to one end and that a blue/black neutral wire is connected to the other end of each element – this aspect is extremely important so check and double check this as you go.

Once cleaning and visual checks have been done, and you are as confident as possible that your components are in good condition (no clear signs of burn-outs of connectors or other damage), then you can start to position your elements into place. I find it helps to first place one end of the element through the hole leading to the electrical panel and have the rest of the element over my shoulder. This means I can then feed the element into its housing before pushing the other end of the element through its second hole leading to the electrical panel. Of course, exactly how you do this will change

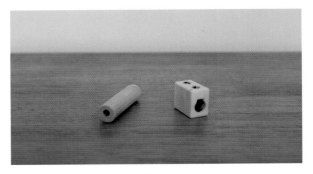

Lead-in tube on the left, ceramic-cased electrical connector on the right. (See the preceding images for information about the placement of these in the control box.)

depending on whether or not you are using a top- or front-loading kiln, as well as the kiln's size. Some kilns have corners and so a kink in the element will be needed to push it into the corner. If buying elements from the manufacturer you will need to make sure these elements line up to the shape of the kiln or, alternatively, you can easily put a small kink in the elements yourself if they arrive without them. Bear in mind this should only be done when the element is brand new and malleable; it is also more easily done when in position inside the kiln.

For barrel-shaped or rounded kilns, having the element a few inches too long for the circumference that it is expected to navigate is a good idea as this means it will brace against the kiln bricks at the back of its housing – a new element can be stretched easily prior to positioning if necessary. Doing this is a little awkward in terms of making the element fit in the first place but it plays its part in preventing sagging elements down the line.

Once an element has been positioned inside the kiln chamber then it is time to position your element connectors inside the control box. First of all, check the ceramic lead-in tubes (many kilns do not have lead-in tubes and may just have a simple hole in the brickwork) are in good order, that is, not broken or cracked. If they are broken or cracked they should be replaced but if they are sound, start to thread the connector onto the element.

The connectors should be close to the lead-in tube. This tube protects the hole between the kiln chamber and control box, as well as providing insulation. Bracing the connector against this prevents excess movement of the element inside the kiln chamber, which will happen with the expansion and contraction of the kiln when it is in use.

Make sure there is good contact between the element and the electrical wire within the connector. The way to do this is to open up the screws of the connector as far as they will go, push the electrical wire and element into it fully and then do up the screws of the connector tightly. Alternatively, if you have a system that requires insulating rings then brace this (with element attached) against the element before crimping it tightly with pliers. Remember the connector should be braced against the lead-in tube or lead-in hole.

At this point, depending on the length of excess Kanthal wire at the end of your new elements, you may need to snip the end of your element short so it protrudes no more than 3–4cm from the connector. This excess wire can then be used by cutting it into 5–7cm lengths that are bent and turned into securing-pins for the elements inside the kiln chamber, as discussed earlier.

Once the above steps are completed, with all connectors replaced and tightly done up, the elements trimmed, with the kiln chamber and control box vacuumed and closed back up, your elements have been and now needed to be tested using the burn test.

THE BURN TEST

At this point we need to test the elements with a burn test. This test can also be used to determine if an element has gone. To do this, some paper of around 10 × 10cm will be needed to slot into a small area on each element. Once you have slotted the paper into each element, close the kiln and

The elements are set up with paper tucked into their housing ready for the burn test.

After around twenty minutes this is what each piece of paper should look like if each element is working correctly.

set the kiln's programmer to go up fast – around 250°C p/h – but with an intention to stop the kiln in around twenty minutes. The kiln temperature does not need to go up very high and, in fact, it is better that it does not; all we are looking for is the heat in the elements to burn the paper slightly. After twenty minutes, shut down the kiln, open the lid or door and look at the pieces of paper. If they all have burn marks then your elements are working. If one or more pieces of paper are not burnt then you may have a connection issue with one of your elements and further diagnosis will be needed or, if using it to see if an element has gone, this will tell you which one. If you have just replaced your elements, then look at the connections for your elements again.

If looking online for information about changing elements or any other aspect of your kiln please be aware that there are different rules and regulations that apply to different countries and so the hardware that will be available in one territory may not be available in another. These differing rules are there for good reasons around compatibility of electrical supply so please do take care to only follow advice appropriate to the country where your kiln is based. All above advice is based on UK regulations.

BRICKWORK

The brickwork in your kiln plays one of the most important roles in your kiln in terms of the insulation it provides, thereby allowing the kiln to reach very high temperatures. It used to be more common for kiln walls to be very thick in order to insulate well but now they are habitually much thinner as their efficiency has increased with improvements in the technology. However, this can mean they are more vulnerable to damage and losing some of their insulating properties if they crack badly or are damaged in some way.

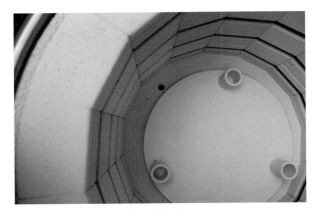
An example of excellent kiln brickwork.

KILN CEMENT

Kiln cement can be bought from ceramic suppliers as a ready-made paste designed to be used to fix the brickwork inside a kiln. Sometimes small cracks will appear in the brickwork but these are normal wear and tear that occurs over time. However, larger cracks or chunks of brickwork coming away, particularly below elements, may need repairing. These jobs can be done by using kiln cement, which effectively acts like a glue or filler. In my own experience the chunk of brickwork that has made a bid for freedom below an element is the highest priority because leaving this unfixed can be like inviting an element to sag into the gap. Simply take the escaped chunk of firebrick and daub the broken surface/s with kiln cement, then hold it in place for a few minutes and it will stay in place. Try to make sure there is enough cement in there to grip on the porous surfaces so do not be shy with the application. A close fit is important so if a little material squeezes out the sides then that is okay as it can be wiped away but make sure that no cement comes into contact with any elements as this will disrupt its oxidized surface. If you are fixing a brick close to an element, putting in place a simple, lightweight barrier is a good idea – for example a sheet of plastic or other tool that is flexible and lifts the element away from the area of work.

CERAMIC FIBRE

Ceramic fibre can be used in the kiln for extra insulation around the base of a kiln, if there are no elements or vents present, and around the lid or door (if appropriate). It has other uses in the kiln but these are the principal occasions that studio-based ceramicists will use it in terms of maintenance in the kiln. If the base of your kiln has a small crack, or you suspect you have an insulation issue in this area, which is visible because of items under-firing, then it is possible to buy sheets of ceramic fibre that can be cut to size and placed in the base of the kiln to improve this situation. It should be noted that heat differences in a kiln chamber can be caused by several problems of which insulation is just one possibility.

Ceramic fibre can be bought in various thicknesses so make sure you have the right one for the job. It is possible to double up if you need more or to add to it if the fibre becomes thin over time.

Ceramic fibre can irritate the skin and catch in the throat so wearing protective gloves and a mask when handling it can be helpful to protect from this. Avoid exposed skin coming into contact with it as well.

Measure the area needing to be covered, making sure it avoids contact with elements or covering any vents. Cut the ceramic fibre blanket with a sharp pair of scissors or blade in order to cut it to size. Take care not to crush it when handling, as it is fairly fragile, and lower it into position, tucking it around the edges and making sure it has contact with the brickwork. If there are larger cracks in the brickwork you may feel it is necessary to restore these with a layer of kiln cement before placing the ceramic fibre in the base of the kiln but, if the base is in average-to-good condition, it may not be needed.

If needing to re-insulate the lid/door, some are designed to have ceramic fibre, but many are not, with the design being a close fit rather than a cushioned fit; if your kiln had ceramic fibre around its lid/door originally, or there is evidence that this used to be in place, then this is the green light to go ahead and replace it if it's worn away. First of all, remove any damaged fibre down to the brickwork using a scraper or brush – please do wear a respiratory mask in a well-ventilated area when doing this and have a vacuum cleaner handy to clean up afterwards. If you can (or have an assistant), hold the vacuum nozzle close to the site where work is taking place as it happens in order to get rid of as much dust as possible before it becomes airborne. A full clean can only take place once the dust has settled so take a break after this job and return a little later to fully vacuum the area, including the site where the new fibre will be positioned.

Then use a scraper to apply a thin layer (approximately 2mm) of kiln cement directly onto the kiln bricks where the fibre is intended to be placed. Once this is done the ceramic fibre that has been cut to size – or, even better, bought as an exactly sized replacement part from the manufacturer of the kiln – can be placed onto the kiln cement and pressed in evenly by hand. Then, very importantly, press the lid/door shut firmly with all clips closed to create the closest fit possible. As I say, it is important to create a thin layer of cement that will not impede the shutting of the lid/door as this can require some force even without excess thickness. The lid/door, once clipped shut, should be left shut for a few hours while the cement goes off and hardens. Please note that insulating your lid/door like this is only necessary if replacing worn-down ceramic fibre and, if the kiln was not originally designed to have it, then the rest of the hardware on the kiln will not fit this extra layer.

CHAPTER 7

BEFORE SETTING UP A KILN IN YOUR OWN STUDIO

Before buying or setting up a kiln in the workshop there are a few 'big picture' realities that need to be considered, such as the type and position of the kiln/s in terms of electricity supply, ventilation and volume of kiln firings. For the most part, how we set up a kiln for our practice will have a compromise somewhere so some thought about what we are prepared to compromise on and what is most important for our creative intentions prior to installing is essential.

JUST ONE KILN?

So much about the type and size of the kiln we choose is down to the equation of space plus budget. However, if you have a large space *and* a large budget it is not always the best option to go big on the size of your kiln. This is because the time it will take to make enough for a full kiln load may be so great that we end up running kilns that are not well packed in order to see results more quickly, so a smaller kiln may be better. A large budget could be seen as an opportunity to buy two kilns of very different sizes in order to have even greater flexibility within our practices. The ecology of our kiln firings should be an important question on our minds when we set up a studio. Older kilns that

are inefficiently insulated should be seriously questioned for their benefits and pitfalls. The technology of kilns has improved hugely with time so I do feel that we should buy the best that we can afford in this sense. Whilst ceramics as an activity has a wholesome reputation it is also hugely energy-hungry and we should never forget this – when buying our kiln, when maintaining it for best efficiency and when packing it well for a firing.

If you are starting from scratch and are very early on in your practice then I would advise a single, small-to-medium-sized electric kiln, at least initially, with a view to evolving your set-up later if needed. If you are more experienced then the volume of work you intend to produce must take precedence in terms of leading your decisions about choice of kiln, but studio space available, as well as the electricity supply that serves it, will play important roles in your decision.

Many ceramicists continue to work with just one kiln to fire all their work throughout their careers by finely balancing all needs through one piece of kit. This has been the way that I have worked for my entire practice and is largely down to my training, when all kilns available at art college would be used for most types of firing; my philosophy has been to do the same in my studio, running all firings through only one kiln. If choosing this method then take care

Choker Vases by Jo Davies.

to ensure your kiln fires to the highest temperature you need as there are many kilns that will only fire to earthenware temperatures, which is fine if this is all you want but is a detail that can be easily missed.

Some ceramicists, such as Katharina Klug, who specializes in working with porcelain, have several kilns to service their studio practice. Katharina grew up seeing her ceramicist mother work to great effect with several kilns in a large studio space, each for different types of firings, and so this is the way that has made most sense for her own practice. One kiln is used for bisq only, one for glaze only, plus there is a small kiln for glaze tests or short deadlines. The benefits of doing this are because higher-temperature stoneware firings are harder on kilns so they need higher-grade, more expensive components. Having a dedicated, perhaps less expensive or lower-quality, kiln purely for bisq (particularly low bisq) will extend the life of the better kiln used exclusively for stoneware glaze firings because it removes this workload from the kiln that is vital to the finishing touches of the ware, that is, the glazing process. Having this discrepancy between two kilns – a very basic kiln for bisq and a more sophisticated kiln for glaze – represents the importance of each type of firing and hints at the budgets that should be reserved for each if your pattern of firing is low bisq then stoneware glaze. *See* Katharina Klug's Maker Profile for a wider description of these working practices.

If choosing to give each kiln a clear use – bisq kiln, glaze kiln, and so on – it is worth considering the accuracy of the kilns in question and allocating their roles accordingly. The kiln will need to be a more sophisticated piece of kit to accommodate great temperature accuracy, or even a complex kiln programme, such as the ones used for crystalline glazes where controlled cooling is required; the better kiln should therefore be used for the glaze firings. Remember that accuracy should also be measured in evenness of temperature throughout the kiln chamber and this can be determined through the use of pyrometric cones.

We may also decide that some glaze materials require 'quarantining' in one kiln. This is certainly the case with chromium oxide, which creates a grey-green colour when used as a glaze or clay-body addition. The reason for this is that it is prone to creating a pink blush or speckles across other items in the kiln but can also build up in the kiln over time; it has a higher toxicity than most other ceramic materials in kiln firings too so any kiln using this should have very good ventilation. Another, albeit less volatile, material is cobalt, which can 'jump' onto other items in the kiln chamber at high temperatures, creating cobalt spots in unwanted places. For this reason, separation from items with cobalt can be desirable.

Another reason to have more than one kiln would be to allow for a faster rate of production with multiple kilns running at once or in relay. Another reason would be to essentially give yourself a spare kiln. This is useful because kilns can be prone to break down so being left without one when up against a deadline is quite stressful. This may be a particular problem if a studio is based in a very rural location where finding an alternative kiln nearby is less easy.

However, it may be decided that a single kiln is the way to go simply because there is no space for another one or the budget does not allow it. Availability of space is the most basic guiding principle in the parameters we give ourselves and all discussions of the above are academic in the face of this. It has certainly been a major factor in the several studios I have worked from during my professional life and so a single kiln is a habit for my practice. We can do many things to protect our kilns from wear and tear, and our work from contamination or from kiln malfunctions as outlined above, but, at the end of the day, space and budget are our absolute parameters when deciding on the nature of our kiln set-up.

TOP LOADER OR FRONT LOADER?

When you have decided on whether you need just one or several kilns it is time to consider whether to go for a front- or top-loading kiln, or a combination. A front-loading kiln, as the name suggests, allows the ceramic items to be loaded from the front of the kiln using a traditional, vertically hung door mechanism. A top-loading kiln has a lid, usually hinged, sometimes with hydraulic struts, allowing kiln packing from the top of the kiln chamber. Front-loading kilns have been seen as more durable historically and it is not uncommon to see kilns of this variety that have given thirty years of service, with good maintenance. Top loaders tend to be lighter weight and have historically been seen as less resilient although their durability seems to have increased proportionately with their popularity in recent years. This is also partly because they are more easily moved from one studio to another – a great benefit in times of short leases and changeable lives.

Top-loading kilns give more internal kiln-chamber space for less external size than their front-loading cousins. Top loaders do this by having thinner insulating walls than front-loading kilns. This has an impact on the cooling rate of a firing, which may be more or less of an issue depending on your creative intentions.

Maximizing chamber size can be especially important in areas where space is at a premium, like an inner-city studio. Top-loading kilns also tend to be on wheels, allowing extra flexibility of position, for instance in order to roll your kiln to the side when not in use or out into the centre of the space when firing. Their relative weight-to-size ratio makes them a little more portable too, which I have found useful when moving studio several times in my early career. This can be a particular issue in London where creative studios are promoted in buildings ear-marked for residential development in a few years and a previously inexpensive studio

Front-loading kiln on left, top-loading kiln on right.

space is given notice when the property developers are finally ready to move in.

My personal attitude to front-loading kilns has been that a good degree of certainty about my studio is required before investing in one, at least one that is big enough to be the one kiln for my entire practice, as outlined above. This has never quite been the case so I have predominantly gone with top-loading kilns.

Anecdotally, the choice of top- or front-loading kiln also seems to be something that has fallen along generational lines; I feel that an older generation of potters who were luckily able to buy property, or invest in the building of studios and even wood-firing kilns, early in their careers had this certainty. Large, front-loading kilns could happily be the norm in these circumstances. Your choice of kiln is not only impacted by the intentions of your creativity but by the local politics of your area: equipment can be moulded to suit either the temporary or the long term so take care to consider this aspect in your choices.

ELECTRICITY SUPPLY

If you have moved into a studio that has three-phase electricity and an isolator switch already in place then congratulations! You are in an ideal situation. Not only will you have a wide choice of kilns but you will have relatively low costs associated with your installation. Three-phase kilns tend to be cheaper per cubic foot than their plug-in and single-phase cousins, which often cost more due to their convenience of installation.

If installing a kiln from scratch, that is, with no electricity supply to the space/studio where you intend to put your kiln, you will need to check that the nearest supply into the main building/house is up to contemporary standards, with all electrical hardware being capable of drawing the required amount of electricity, especially if firing to stoneware temperatures. This can be assessed by an electrician but, if in the UK, UK Power Networks can also assess aspects of your supply for you.

When I built a separate studio building at my last property, setting up its electricity supply did involve upgrading the 60amp fuse supplying my home to 100amp because of the kiln. This was a job that was done for free by UK Power Networks ahead of any further electrical work being undertaken. Many residential buildings have a 60amp fuse but 100amp fuses are increasingly common in modern homes with some going up to 200amp – unfortunately I had inherited a very old system so an update way beyond just the fuse was required. Each situation is different so a free site visit by UK Power Networks is well worth arranging.

If your electrical supply is up to the standard for the energy needed by the kiln you have, or the one you want, then you are in a good position. I would advise that this can only be fully evaluated by your electrician so consult with them before buying a kiln.

Try to find a position for the kiln in the studio, ahead of placing all other furniture and equipment, through conversations with your electrician and/or other professional. If supplying a shed/building with a new electricity supply then this should be designed to reach you by the easiest way possible – this usually means close to an existing supply or at a point that requires the shortest length of cable, taking into account all safety considerations and current legislation.

VENTILATION FOR KILNS

Ventilation and space for airflow around the kiln is another important factor when positioning your kiln because kilns give off a large amount of heat and, depending on what is being fired, fumes and gases. These fumes can be particularly pungent in the first half of the firing. Many kilns at institutions like universities or schools tend to have full ventilation hoods and extraction to remove gases and heat away from workshops and offices adjacent to them. This is

An example of ventilation for a kiln. Kiln ventilation can be designed in many different ways.

My kiln shed with door closed.

My kiln shed open and housing a top-loading Potclays kiln.

something that can be installed in a commercial or home studio too. In some situations, however, it is a sledgehammer to crack a nut. One of the reasons this is the case is that the frequency of firings will be lower in an individual ceramicist's studio than in an institution serving the firing needs of many students, so try to predict how often you intend to fire. In reality, even professional potters only average three to six firings per month across a year and hooded ventilation systems are extremely expensive on top of your kiln costs.

It is important to remember that the main function of a ventilation system is to allow the people in residence, or at work, to go about their daily business in the same or adjacent space to a kiln without breathing fumes coming from it. As an alternative,

ventilation can be achieved by having the kiln in a separate building or shed that is away from home or workshop, with its window or door open. Of course, everyone's situation is different and you may feel that this is a security risk in your circumstances, or you may not have the space. However, if ventilation can be achieved through a separate position, in a building that is not where people work or live, then a hooded ventilation system with extraction is not required. This simpler option enables the dissipation of heat and gases and is all that is needed. Even the most expensive extraction system will only vent into the open air adjacent to the space so look at the position of the kiln itself as part of solving the problem of ventilation.

If opting for a separate building in which to house a kiln, it should have approximately 18in (45cm) around it in all directions to allow for heat circulation so this would mean that, depending on the size of kiln you have, a separate building may only need to be a weatherproof shed. At my own home studio I have opted to have a kiln shed built for this purpose. My studio space is separated inside the main house, which is a much warmer situation than many other studios I have occupied, but does mean that loading a kiln is a little more of an event than if it is inside the workshop. There are pros and cons to this set-up but it is preferable to the kiln being inside the main house because I avoid fumes and excess heat inside.

When deciding on a place for your kiln, whether this is in the studio or a separate space, consider if there are any flammable materials contained within the infrastructure of the walls nearby. If you have a lot of wood around then this is not necessarily an end to that position because you can make sure there is a decent gap between kiln and wood or clad the walls immediately adjacent with, for instance, a fire-resistant plasterboard or other non-flammable material that does not have good heat transfer.

If you have your studio at home, my instinct is to avoid a kiln inside the main house if possible. If you cannot avoid this then I recommend having an excellent hooded ventilation system put in place along with all fire safety precautions and electrical fail-safes. This is also necessary if placing a kiln in a commercial premises that has other businesses adjacent to it.

Contemporary kilns have several ways to turn themselves off if things go wrong; many malfunctions will automatically cut the kiln's electrical circuit, resulting in the kiln simply turning itself off. In many ways the least likely thing to happen is that a kiln starts a fire if something goes wrong inside it but this does not mean we should throw caution to the wind because it does sometimes happen. If setting up a kiln inside a residential property, all precautions of this nature should be observed and firing at night, when people and pets are sleeping, should be completely avoided.

However, if you occupy a studio alone, and the space is not attached to any other property, then ask yourself if the kiln can be placed inside the studio space itself. This is a solution if you are happy to not work in the studio while the kiln is firing but can check on it. This is by far the most common way for individual ceramicists to work.

The author at work in her studio.

CHAPTER 8

BUYING KILNS

Buying a kiln can be a slightly daunting task if doing this for the first time. There are many different varieties and styles of kiln so doing your research as well as having a clear idea of your intentions for your practice is very important. This chapter is a general guide to be used in conjunction with information available from manufacturers and professionals like electricians who would be involved in your installation.

START WITH THE ELECTRICITY SUPPLY AND WORK BACKWARDS

A mistake often made is to buy a kiln before understanding the electrical parameters in the studio setting available, that is, a kiln is bought and the electrical fittings are made to fit, sometimes awkwardly. It is certainly possible for this to work out well but knowing the actual parameters of the site beforehand is better. When you know this, and have some idea of your individual creative intentions, you are ready to put money down on a kiln. The kiln should serve the ceramics practitioner using it, rather than the kiln calling the shots because its capabilities do not quite fit your plan.

Ahead of choosing a kiln, whether it is second hand or brand new, you should have worked out how you will power it. Kilns for studio-based ceramics are powered in three different ways: plug-in, single-phase and three-phase. Plug-in kilns, as the name suggests, are set up with a domestic plug and are small; single-phase kilns are small-to-medium-sized and need to be hardwired to the fuse box; three-phase kilns are medium-to-large kilns and require hardwiring to the fuse box in addition to a bolstered electricity supply coming into the property. Many kilns in a mid-size can be powered with either single- or three-phase electricity.

Having a kiln that needs to be hardwired to the fuse box does not always mean that we need to have a three-phase electricity supply and many very reasonably sized kilns are happy with single-phase electricity, which amounts to an ordinary domestic supply. However, your supply would need at least a 100amp fuse to function – which is now very often the standard in UK homes but lower fuses are still common so, if you are considering a home studio, this will be important to establish. Commercial premises often have three-phase supplying them, or at least a single-phase supply with a 100amp fuse. Either way, it is worth checking and this can be easily done through UK Power Networks who offer site visits for properties to assess the fuse you have and if you need upgrading. A phone call to your landlord or electrician may also tell you all you need to know

Speak Vase with Two by Jo Davies.

about this in the first instance. Please also note that upgrading may mean some of the surrounding hardware on the fuse board will need to be changed by either your electrician or electricity company but UK Power Networks can assess the site and let you know if this is the case. Contacting UK Power Networks will be a starting point in working out your situation and you may find that you can install without any issue or significant changes.

PLUG-IN KILNS

Plug-in kilns are designed with a domestic plug to be used with an ordinary domestic socket and electricity supply – they are very tempting for ease of use because theoretically no preparation or professional help in setting the kiln up is needed. However, they tend to have small kiln chambers and do not always work well in certain circumstances.

Plug-in kilns can serve well but, in my experience as well as anecdotally, they struggle at stoneware temperatures unless they are very good-quality kilns or brand new. *See* Helen Johannessen's Maker Profile for an example of a studio that operates successfully with a plug-in kiln at stoneware temperatures. However, it can often be the case for plug-in kilns to struggle to draw enough electricity through domestic wiring in the stoneware temperature range. If plug-in kilns do not have good enough insulation and/or heat transfer from their elements because of age or another reason, they will struggle to go to stoneware temperatures. This is partly because they cannot hold onto the heat inside the chamber while simultaneously providing sufficient power through their elements to achieve these temperatures. As mentioned, the draw of electricity can be the main issue with these kilns so, if this is a problem for your plug-in kiln, then a conversation with your electrician may be useful in improving things. However, if you only intend to use the kiln within the earthenware range then a plug-in will often tolerate electrical supplies that are not perfect. Personally, I am a little uncomfortable with the idea of plug-in kilns as they give the impression that they can be placed anywhere, in any environment and with any socket, but the truth is that the amount of electricity needed to be drawn, as well as the placement of the kiln, should be managed better than this. The design and construction of most plug-in kilns is, no doubt, very good when new but it relies on the electrical supply and wiring of their setting to be excellent.

SINGLE-PHASE KILNS

There are many decent-sized kilns that will run on a single-phase, domestic electricity supply (*see* information above). There may be a perceived inconvenience in hardwiring a kiln to the fuse box with an isolator switch but this can actually make the supply more reliable and safe therefore making your firings run well.

If you have opted for a single-phase kiln it will need to be hardwired to the fuse box with a single, heavy-duty cable along with an isolator switch close to the kiln. This is a job for an electrician. However, the cost of this service can be significantly less than installing three-phase electricity and still gives you a good-sized kiln. Personally, I believe that a hardwired kiln at single-phase is a better option for a home studio or small commercial space than a plug-in kiln. It is often assumed that three-phase electricity is always needed if you want a kiln that is larger than a plug-in but this is not the case. The expense of installing a three-phase electricity supply from scratch can go into thousands of pounds, with the final cost of this depending on many factors, so do also look at kilns that are listed as being able to run on either single- or three-phase electricity supply.

An example of an isolator switch.

We can see here that the kiln has its own fuse on the far right in this domestic setting.

At the bottom right-hand corner of this kiln's label we can see that next to 'Phase' it says '1 or 3'. This means that this kiln will run on either single- or three-phase electricity.

THREE-PHASE KILNS

A three-phase supply is often necessary for very large kilns. In a nutshell, 'three phase' amounts to a boost in your electricity supply that requires extra cables into your workshop and into the kiln itself. Many mid-sized kilns can be supplied by either single- or three-phase electricity supplies so there is flexibility in this but large kilns will definitely need a three-phase supply. The kiln itself should have a label on or near its control box that states its make and model, serial number, maximum temperature, its voltage, kilowatt hours and, importantly, whether it requires either single- or three-phase electricity, or if it can be run on either. Again, a conversation can be started with UK Power Networks about setting up a bolstered, three-phase electricity supply as they would be the organization overseeing the installation of this into the premises, if needed. Like I say, researching what you have in terms of electricity supply before buying any kiln will help you to budget properly.

As part of determining which kiln to buy, a conversation with your electrician at the property in which you intend to house the kiln will help you to work out what you have available already, what can be done within budget and if any additional work is needed. There was a time when kilns that can now be supplied by single-phase electricity could only be supplied by three-phase. However, as our electricity use as a society has increased, so has the domestic supply into our properties, and running an average-sized kiln in a home workshop or commercial premises on just single-phase is therefore not quite the problem it once was. Having said this, this is as long as you do not run the oven, microwave, washing machine, fridge/freezer, every TV in the house and every other electricity-hungry device you own all at the same point as the kiln is reaching temperature – much like Wi-Fi bandwidth, there is a limit.

In my own practice, I have found that a kiln rated as being able to run on either single- or three-phase gives me enough capacity. I acquired my Potclays top-loading kiln second-hand a few years ago. Its chamber size is 65cm diameter × 50cm height and it can be run using single- or three-phase electricity, but I run it using single-phase. I run the kiln to stoneware temperatures up to 1,260°C with a soak so, in terms of temperature, it achieves almost the maximum it would need to achieve for a ceramic kiln. It has been hardwired to my domestic fuse box and runs without issue. My kiln is not the largest I have seen that will run with single-phase so it is worth investigating the size of kilns available within this bracket and working out your requirements before going to the expense of a larger kiln. Of course, if you have a studio with three-phase already in place then your choices are maximized.

CREATIVE INTENTIONS

In deciding on your kiln, really consider the following: what you want to make, your volume of production, the frequency of firings required and temperature range. You may only be able to answer one or two of these considerations; that is fine – just try to allow yourself scope for flexibility if there are uncertainties.

Kiln technology is ever evolving so research thoroughly and do not be afraid to ask professional kiln doctors and electricians for their advice; use their expertise when necessary. Electricians, even if they have not dealt with kilns before, should be able to understand the electrical requirements needed by them so please do also speak with an electrician you may already know rather than waiting for months for the kiln-specialist electrician to be available. By seeking as much advice before buying you will end up really drilling down into what is necessary for you and the practicalities of the situation of your studio, which will save you a lot of money and time in the end.

If you are uncertain about exactly what you would like to do creatively then my advice is to go for a kiln that is capable of stoneware temperatures so you have the greatest scope and are not just limited to earthenware clays and glazes (some kilns are designed to only reach earthenware). Also, do not be tempted to buy a very large kiln in the first instance, unless you know you want to make large things or know that you will be producing volume. The reason for this is that it can be better, in those first steps, to have a kiln that does not take too long to fill before a firing as well as considering the issues mentioned around electricity supply of these large kilns. At the beginning of your practice, by having a small-to-medium-sized kiln, you can pack the kiln well after a short time, run it efficiently and,

crucially, see frequent results rather than waiting a long time between firings, thereby speeding up your learning and development. Even if you have the kiln hardwired, after a while, a new one of a larger size (up to a point) can very often replace it with only the wiring up to the isolator switch needing to be replaced. It is even possible that this could be reused too but this should be dealt with under advice from a professional assessing the individual situation.

Whatever you decide to do, the help and advice from your local electrician, kiln doctor and kiln manufacturer will be very useful before buying anything. Having an understanding of the electrical supply you have will save you a lot of heartache so please do take advice on your individual circumstances before buying anything.

CHAPTER 9

BUYING SECOND-HAND KILNS

Buying a second-hand kiln can be a great way to save money. At one end of the quality spectrum there are often kilns on the second-hand market that have hardly been used – originally bought for a hobby, they are no longer needed when enthusiasm wanes and so end up being sold again, albeit a few years later, but with only a handful of firings on the clock. This is the best situation for a relatively new ceramicist looking to save some money *and* have a quality kiln.

Another possibility is that you find a kiln that has been owned by an institution, college or university. These are interesting prospects as the seller does not necessarily have as strong an interest in the price they gain; the kiln will have been used an average-to-heavy amount but, crucially, they will, if all protocols were taken, have been professionally serviced every year throughout their life. Parts will have been renewed before absolutely necessary and maintenance is likely to have been decent. This makes this source of kiln another strong prospect for a fledgling ceramicist but do ask for a written history of its maintenance certificates.

A little further down the spectrum are kilns that have been well used by a professional potter but may or may not have been well looked after. They will have more marks of use and a little more

rust; they may also have been second hand when they were bought although some kilns can reach an age of a few decades if looked after well. These prospects require a little more examination and some caution should be employed before buying. Asking why someone is selling is always a good idea. A professional may want to renew because the kiln is no longer as accurate as it once was or there is a need for more automation and therefore a higher specification kiln, or perhaps they need a bigger or smaller kiln instead. If the answer is around accuracy then ask yourself how much accuracy your practice will need – for instance, perhaps this is a kiln for bisq rather than glaze if you have space for multiple kilns?

At the very end of the second-hand kiln spectrum there are 'barn finds'. These kilns have often been sitting for years inside someone's barn or shed, unloved and unused. Very often the person selling it may not know what to do with it, anything about it or whether it fires. They may have inherited it from a great aunt and are finally coming around to selling it and making space. These kilns tend to go for a very cheap price or are even free so are often tempting to new ceramicists. The problem with these kilns is that they very often do not work and need some expertise to get them up and running

Original Twist Pendant by Jo Davies.

again. There is also the cost of moving them. A top-loading kiln can be moved into a van or car with the help of a few people but many front-loading kilns, because of their bulkier size and shape, can be very difficult indeed to move and this cost can rack up to a few hundred pounds when considering van hire (a tail-lift version may be needed) and hire of other moving equipment and/or expertise. So, on the occasions when you may be offered a free or cheap kiln, consider the cost of lifting, transporting and fixing to make it work before going ahead. The time, money and inconvenience are quite surprising if you are new to ceramics and, if the aim is to fire clay, experiment and move forward creatively then spend what will inevitably be the same amount

of money on a kiln you know works that can be transported in a car or van, preferably with two or three people to move it by hand. However, if you are interested in the challenge of making kilns work, their engineering, and restoring these items for fun or even for resale then these are great options.

Very importantly please bear in mind that there was a time when much older kilns (up until the 1970s) were being made with asbestos as part of their insulating walls. This tended to be the case for front-loading kilns more than top-loading ones but, if considering an older kiln, it is worth researching the age, make and model to work out if that kiln has asbestos as part of its walls and insulation – a phone call to the original manufacturer may help

SECOND-HAND KILN CHECKLIST OF CONDITION

- Does it fire to the temperature range you require? Many kilns are only graded to earthenware temperatures and will not reach stoneware so double check this before everything else.
- Brickwork – is it sound and uncracked? If there are some cracks, how structural are they? If only small and superficial then this is passable and possibly just a negotiating point.
- Elements – do they have a very, very pitted surface? Are they misshapen and sagging from their housing? If yes to both they are likely to be quite old and need changing. Again, this can be a negotiating point as it will be an extra cost to you when you have the kiln.
- Can the seller offer a recent receipt for replacement elements/parts, or certificate for recent work or service by a professional? It may be worth asking for this ahead of visiting.
- Rust – is there rust all around the lid/door or the vents and elsewhere? If there is a lot it either indicates that the kiln has not been cared for or that the firings have been run habitually with wet items in the chamber. This is an indicator that there will be more rust elsewhere in contacts and connectors. However, it is common for there to be some rust in these areas; it should just not be excessive.
- Ask to see it turning on. Say you would like to see

this ahead of arriving to view the kiln, as sometimes a seller will undo the wiring ahead of time for speed, but it is worth asking for this and hearing those reassuring clicks.
- What is the lid/door fit like? Is it flush with the rest of the kiln? If it is off then you may end up with an insulation issue.
- Is the lid/door hinging mechanism good? Ideally a smooth-closing mechanism is ideal to avoid disruptive movement of the kiln once it is packed. This may read like a small thing but is critical with anything light or if using certain types of setters or stilts.
- Try to look underneath the kiln – does the brickwork have good structural integrity?
- Does the price include any pieces of kiln furniture? Are they in good condition and not covered in glaze drips or pockmarks?
- Does it include the kiln programmer? If so, check that this is working and that its connection to the kiln's control box is sound.

Ultimately, it is difficult to truly assess a kiln's accuracy and firing capability before it arrives back in the studio and is tested but the above will give some indication of performance.

you work this out if they are still in business. These kilns are fine if continuing to be used *in situ* and not moved but, as with all asbestos, the movement is what disturbs it and makes it dangerous. Bearing this in mind, moving kilns made in that era is either a specialist job involving licensed professionals or one to just avoid altogether because of the serious health risks associated with asbestos. If deciding to go ahead with a kiln like this then evaluate how long you intend to be in the workshop you are moving it to. If it is going to be a long time then it may be worth it but if your space is in any way under question then a more 'mobile' prospect would be better. Also, resale or disposal of these items can be tricky so make sure the kiln you are considering is worth the effort.

CHECKLIST OF POTENTIAL EXTRA COSTS

- Transport of the kiln – simple van hire, a van with a tail lift or professional movers?
- The cost of an electrician hardwiring the kiln at your studio
- The cost of wire and other electrical materials from fuse box to kiln plus isolator switch
- Ventilation – *see* the section on 'Ventilation for Kilns' in Chapter 7 as you may or may not need this.
- Kiln furniture and kiln props
- Delivery of the kiln furniture and props
- Cost of kiln doctor and spare parts if work is needed on a second hand kiln

This list will vary depending on the kiln, your situation and your creative intentions. However, it is best to use this list in order to check if any are covered within the quoted cost of the kiln but, if not, research what each of these will cost before committing to the kiln.

WHERE TO LOOK

When searching for second-hand kilns the usual online places are still some of the best places – eBay, Gumtree and so on; Facebook Marketplace as well as the various pottery/ceramics groups on there are useful, some of which are set up specifically for buying and selling ceramic equipment. If you are not time pressured then set up an email alert on eBay and other sites for items fitting your needs so that anything that may be of interest is sent to your inbox.

Local pottery groups may also be good sources of kit so it is always worth asking there too. Sometimes these groups are mainly offline, or not well updated online, so accessing them may be a phone call away, a visit to a local ceramics supplier may help or even just joining the group as a member. I have also known kiln doctors to buy and sell second-hand kilns. This can be an excellent option because they may have looked over the kiln and brought it up to speed before putting it up for sale again but double check this before assuming as they may also just be acting as a go-between for ceramicists.

Of course, the simple act of asking if there are any kilns available amongst friends – both online or offline – can also gain results because you may find kilns that have not yet reached the market and so a bargain can be had from someone who was considering selling but is happy to sell cheaper because of the convenience of selling without hassle or sales fees.

There can be a strong market for second-hand kilns and it can be competitive to buy one so the more obscure your source the less competition there will be. This is particularly the case if you are prepared to travel to remote areas to collect a kiln.

When buying a second-hand kiln, one of the best things you can do is to give yourself time to look and consider – both the situation where the kiln is intended to be housed as well as the kiln itself.

SUPPLIERS

Corby Kilns
www.corbykilns.co.uk

Essex Kilns Ltd
www.essexkilns.co.uk

Kilns & Furnaces Ltd
www.kilns.co.uk

Clayman Supplies Limited
www.claymansupplies.co.uk

Potclays Limited
www.potclays.co.uk

Bath Potters Supplies
www.bathpotters.co.uk

CTM Potters Supplies
www.ctmpotterssupplies.co.uk

Northern Kilns
www.northernkilns.com

Nabertherm Kilns
www.nabertherm.com

Kittec
https://kittec.eu

L&L Kilns
www.hotkilns.com

Cromartie Hobbycraft Limited
www.cromartiehobbycraft.co.uk

Potterycrafts Ltd
www.potterycrafts.co.uk

AMERICAN SUPPLIERS

American Ceramic Supply Company
www.americanceramics.com

Clay King
www.clay-king.com

Ceramic Supply Pittsburgh
https://ceramicsupplypittsburgh.com

CONTRIBUTORS

Jo Davies

Jo Davies is a ceramicist specializing in wheel-thrown porcelain. She has a ceramics degree from Bath School of Art & Design and Masters in ceramics from the Royal College of Art. She exhibits and sells her work nationally and

internationally, notably she has worked with the National Portrait Gallery, Yorkshire Sculpture Park, Heals and the Contemporary Ceramics Centre, as well as a solo exhibition at the Mufei Gallery in Shanghai. She also has a private teaching practice that specializes in wheel-throwing. Jo Davies studio images are by Matthew Booth, Dan Barker, Tim Jobling with additional workshop images by the artist.

www.jo-davies.com

Tessa Eastman

Tessa Eastman is a ceramic sculptor living and working in London. She has a Ceramics Degree from the University of West-minster as well as a Masters from the Royal

College of Art. She has an international reputation away from her UK home, notably exhibiting with Jason Jacques Gallery in New York, Galerie de l'Ancienne Poste in France and the Gyeonggi Ceramic Biennale in Korea to name a few.

Studio Photographs of her sculptures are by Juliet Sheath with other accompanying workshop images by Jo Davies.

www.tessaeastman.com

Katharina Klug

Katharina Klug is a potter based in Cambridge, UK but she is Austrian by birth. Her ceramics practice began early as her mother is also a potter and so Katharina was

informally trained by her from an early age. Her work is exhibited and sold widely through many galleries in the UK and internationally, as well as through her website. Her porcelain has been shown at Heals and The Contemporary Ceramics Centre in London, as well as The Centre of Ceramic Art in York. She has also been supported by Arts Council England with a research grant.

Studio Photographs of her work are by Zuza Grubecka with accompanying workshop images by Jo Davies.

www.katharinaklugceramics.com

Annabel Faraday

Annabel Farraday is a ceramicist based in Fairlight near Hastings in Southern England. She exhibits internationally as well as regularly being commissioned to create unique pieces for

private clients. Annabel is a selected member of the UK Craft Potters Association with work included in the collections of the Potteries Museum, Stoke-on-Trent and the Museum of the Home, London.

Studio photographs of her work are by John Cole with accompanying workshop images by Jo Davies.

www.annabelfaraday.com

Akiko Hirai

Akiko Hirai is a Japanese potter living in London. She is a Fellow of the Craft Potters Association and has frequent solo exhibitions in the UK at prestigious galleries

like The Newcraftsman in St Ives, The Scottish Gallery, Beaux Arts Bath and The Contemporary Ceramics Centre in London. She also has an international reputation and her work is much sought after, frequently selling out at shows and fairs.

Studio photographs of her work are by the artist with all accompanying workshop images by Jo Davies.

www.akikohiraiceramics.com

Helen Johannessen

Helen Johannessen lives in London and started her career in ceramics with her successful brand Yoyo Ceramics in 2000. In 2015 she was accepted

at the Royal College of Art to do her Masters and her work made the leap into sculpture. She has since become an award-winning artist exhibiting and working internationally along with a reputation as a sought after teacher with expertise in plaster mould-making. Studio Photographs of her work are by Chris Evans with accompanying workshop images by Jo Davies.

www.helenjohannessen.co.uk

Jeremy Nichols

Jeremy Nichols originally trained as an aeronautical engineer at Manchester University but then added to this qualification with certificates in social work, embarking

on an 18 year career in this area before gaining a degree in ceramics at the University of Westminster in 1997. He is a regular exhibitor at Ceramic Art London and major exhibitions around the UK as well as frequently showing at international galleries and museums. He is a professional member of the UK Craft Potters Association and the Art Workers Guild. All Jeremy Nichols images are by the artist.

www.jeremynichols.co.uk

Sasha Wardell

Sasha Wardell is a highly accomplished ceramicist working and innovating in the use of Bone China. She has taught at universities across the UK and abroad,

has written several books and has an international reputation for a pioneering approach in making her bone china range of objects. She has exhibited at numerous prestigious exhibitions around the world. Sash Wardell images are by Mark Lawrence.

www.sashawardell.com

Rachel Grimshaw

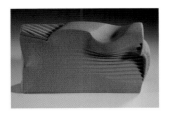

Rachel Grimshaw is an award-winning artist based in Wigan in the North of England. She has an international profile, frequently exhibiting across Europe and beyond. She also complements her time as a ceramicist by working as an interior designer, with each discipline informing one another to make her work what it is. Rachel Grimshaw's image is by Ryan Mullally.

www.rachelgrimshaw.co.uk

Jessica Thorn

Jessica Thorn is based in Bristol in South West England. Having graduated from Plymouth University, she has since been selected to be part of the Crafts Council's Hothouse scheme as well as gaining support

from Arts Council England. She exhibits her unique and distinctive range of slip cast porcelain in galleries and stockists across the UK. Jessica Thorn studio image is by Silkie Lloyd with workshop images by the artist.

www.jessicathorn.co.uk

INDEX

ACKNOWLEDGEMENTS

This book would not have been possible without the kind help of contributors who generously gave their time at their studios, by email and over the phone. Maker Profiles were the product of studio visits when each maker allowed me to take photographs and record interviews with them. Much of their expertise and knowledge has been woven into the main body of the book as well as their individual profiles and I am hugely grateful for their time and help. Akiko Hirai, Katharina Klug, Annabel Faraday, Helen Johannessen and Tessa Eastman all allowed me significant access to their workshops, ideas and making practices as part of the research for this publication.

Other contributors include Jeremy Nichols, whose images and freely given information provided great examples of intricate, intelligently worked out propping techniques.

Jaejun Lee's images of his work have offered beautiful examples of how glaze can be both expertly manipulated and allowed to flow.

Rachel Grimshaw provided images of her beautiful, unorthodox approach to sculpture.

Susan Nemeth was one of my studio neighbours for ten years and generously allowed me to use her images alongside memories of our conversations in the text. Jessica Thorn also provided technical insight along with images of her amazing work so I could illustrate different approaches to glazing.

I would also like to thank Corby Kilns in Kettering for proofreading Chapter 6: Kiln Maintenance and for their patience in allowing me to take up their time with questions and confirmations.

A special thanks goes to The Kiln Rooms open access ceramics studio in South London, but particularly to Sean Bruno for his very important help with some extra photography and sheer generosity of spirit.

And finally, a big thank you to CUP Ceramics Community in Hereford for their warm welcome and for kindly loaning me some of their equipment for photography.

First published in 2022 by
The Crowood Press Ltd
Ramsbury, Marlborough
Wiltshire SN8 2HR

enquiries@crowood.com
www.crowood.com

© Jo Davies 2022

British Library Cataloguing-in-Publication Data
A catalogue record for this book is available from the British Library.

ISBN 978 0 7198 4147 7

Cover design: Sergey Tsvetkov

Disclaimer
Safety is of the utmost importance in every aspect of kiln firing, and the practical workshop procedures are potentially dangerous. The author and publisher cannot accept responsibility for any accident or injury caused by following the advice given in this book.

Graphic design and typesetting by Peggy & Co. Design
Printed and bound in India by Parksons Graphics